DECISION
point

DynamicCatholic.com
Be Bold. Be Catholic.

DECISION POINT: The Leader Guide

In accord with the *Code of Canon Law,* I hereby grant the *Imprimatur* ("Permission to Publish") for *Decision Point.*

> Most Reverend Dennis M. Schnurr
> Archbishop of Cincinnati
> Archdiocese of Cincinnati
> Cincinnati, Ohio
> April 4, 2014

The *Imprimatur* ("Permission to Publish") is a declaration that a book is considered to be free of doctrinal or moral error. It is not implied that those who have granted the Imprimatur agree with the contents, opinions, or statements expressed.

Design by: Shawna Powell
Illustration by: Jenny Miller & Hazel Mitchell

ISBN 978-1-937509-73-6

FIRST EDITION [4]

Acknowledgments

This project began with a dream.

More than seven hundred people have poured their time, talent, and treasure into DECISION POINT. It is the result of years of research, development, and testing. To everyone involved in every stage of the process: Thank you! May God bless you and reward you richly for your generosity.

Now we offer it to the Church as a gift, hopeful that it will help millions of young people encounter Jesus and discover the genius of Catholicism.

Special thanks goes to: Matthew Kiernan, Margie Rapp, Allen Hunt, Anita Hunt, Fr. Robert Sherry, Tim Nowak, Penny Giunta, Beth Rainford, Ashley Berger, and Fr. David Zink.

DECISION POINT was funded by a group of generous donors. It will now be made available at no cost to every parish in North America. This is one of the many ways that this program is unique.

Everything great in history has been accomplished by people who believed that the future could be better than the past. Thank you for believing!

DynamicCatholic.com
Be Bold. Be Catholic.

TABLE of CONTENTS

WELCOME

It began with a dream—to give catechists, youth ministers, sponsors, parents, pastors, and Directors of Religious Education (DREs) the tools they need to engage young Catholics in a meaningful conversation about the genius of Catholicism in preparation for the Sacrament of Confirmation.

Catechesis is the Church's efforts to bring to life the teachings of Jesus Christ in the lives of ordinary men, women, and children. Religious education classes are one of the primary forms of catechesis.

But evangelization precedes catechesis.

Evangelization is first and foremost a dialogue. It is not a monologue. Evangelization is a personal and powerful conversation that leads to conversion of heart, mind, and soul.

And let's face it, our young people need to be evangelized. They need to hear the Gospel in a way that is fresh, intriguing, relevant, compelling, and attractive. Too often we make the mistake of assuming that they have made a choice for Christ and his Church, when the great majority of them have not. They need to be boldly invited to choose Christ and the Church.

The theology of Confirmation informs us that it is about God choosing us, but we are endowed with free will and so for God to do his best work in us and through us we need to respond and cooperate as Mary and the saints did.

It is our hope that this program will not only prepare young Catholics for the Sacrament of Confirmation in a dynamic way, but also teach and inspire them to respond and cooperate with God's grace in all the circumstances of their daily lives, long after their Confirmation has passed.

These materials are the result of thousands of hours of work. More than seven hundred people have been involved in the process. Never before has a Catholic program been developed with such rigorous research, development, and testing. Yes, testing. Over and over again, we have put these materials in front of teens and asked them to tell us what was working and what wasn't. Over and over, we refined our offering based on that feedback.

And we are not finished yet. For decades we have been using programs that were developed once and never changed, or changed every seven years. That is not the case with DECISION POINT. We hope you will provide feedback so that we can continue to improve this offering regularly.

Whatever role you play in preparing young Catholics for Confirmation, we realize it may be a thankless job—so we want to thank you. Thank you for all you are doing for the Church. It is our hope and prayer that this program will help make your experience with today's Catholic teens infinitely more fulfilling for you and for them.

There is a moment in each person's life when our eyes get wide and begin to sparkle. At Dynamic Catholic we call that the "I get it now" moment. We hope that our efforts combined with your dedication will produce more "I get it now" moments for Catholic teens.

May the grace of our abundantly generous God inspire you and give you courage, wisdom, and patience.

•———— The Dynamic Catholic Team ————•

THE DYNAMIC CATHOLIC APPROACH

This is different. One look at the materials for DECISION POINT and that is clear. It looks different because it is different. But it is not just different in how it looks and feels. The way we developed it was very different from how Catholic programs have been developed in the past.

And it's not just different for the sake of being different. It's different for a reason. Let's be honest—the old way isn't working. Eighty-five percent of young Catholics stop practicing their faith within ten years of their Confirmation. Different is needed.

DECISION POINT is different in a hundred ways.

THE PROCESS

Dynamic Catholic was founded on the idea of "meeting people where they are and leading them to where God is calling them to be." Once Catholics are engaged in their spiritual journey, there is an abundance of materials that can feed them and draw them deeper into relationship with God and the Church. But there is a great shortage of materials that engage disengaged Catholics.

Most young Catholics are disengaged. Engaging them is therefore the first step. Until they are engaged it doesn't matter how much information you download on them; they simply will not absorb it and make it their own.

There are many programs that faithfully present the teachings of the Church. But that alone is not enough. While presenting the Church's teachings faithfully is essential, it is also critically important that they be presented in ways that are engaging, accessible, and relevant.

In setting out, our goal was to create the most dynamic program to prepare young Catholics for Confirmation. But we realized that in order to do this we had to get a real sense of what was working, what wasn't working, and what experts on the front lines thought was needed.

DECISION POINT has taken more than four years to develop. The truth is, in many ways it is very different from what we originally envisioned. When we first set out we thought that the entire program would be online. But over and over again, you asked for physical workbooks, leader guides, and DVDs—so we adapted. Hundreds of people have spoken into this project, and it is better because of that.

This is the process we worked through to deliver what you now hold in your hands.

YEAR ONE: LISTEN

We spent the first year just listening. During that time we conducted more than seven hundred interviews with catechists, DREs, priests, youth ministers, youth group leaders, high school and middle school teachers, parents, candidates, current and former sponsors, and bishops.

YEAR TWO: EXPLORE

We spent the second year exploring every Confirmation preparation program that was currently available. We analyzed the differences and similarities between each program. We investigated which parts of each program were effective and which aspects simply weren't working. We also explored best practices among other Christian churches and groups to discover how they were engaging their teens. Then we spent a lot of time asking why. Over and over again, we asked why: Why does this work? Why doesn't this work? Why don't young people respond to this or that? What will it take to really engage them in a meaningful discussion about the genius of Catholicism?

YEAR THREE: DEVELOP AND TEST

By the third year we were developing our own program based on all that we had learned. This began a cycle of development and testing. We would develop snippets of material and then test them with Catholic teens. A lot of the material worked, but some didn't. And all of it was improved by the feedback we got during the testing.

YEAR FOUR: REFINE AND RETEST

In the fourth year we finalized the structure, layout, and content of DECISION POINT, all the time retesting and refining even the smallest details.

Now it's time to share it with the world. But we see the launch of DECISION POINT as just a larger pilot study. We know it isn't perfect; no program is. The difference is, we are not done yet. Many programs get launched and are never changed. But we are excited to continuously improve this program based on the feedback you and your students provide to us. So if you see a typo or a substantial way to improve this program, please let us know.

DECISION POINT IS FOR ALL CATHOLICS

DECISION POINT is a Confirmation preparation program primarily designed for Catholics between the ages of twelve and eighteen. It has been designed to ignite a conversation about the genius of Catholicism between candidates and their parents, sponsors, catechists, teachers, peers, and priests. That conversation will be different if you're teaching this content to a group of middle school students than it would be if you were teaching it to a group of high school seniors. But the nature of the content and questions makes them flexible for a broad age group.

In fact, as you get into the materials, you may have the same reaction that many Confirmation leaders had in our focus groups when they said, "Every Catholic should experience this program—not just teens preparing for Confirmation!"

In response to this feedback we made two significant changes to the program. First, we abandoned the idea of having separate workbooks for parents and sponsors and decided that candidates, parents, and sponsors should all have the same workbook, and that we would make the content that's unique to parents and sponsors available online.

Next, we decided to develop a version of the program that would be available in the form of a weekly e-mail. In this way, parents and sponsors can have an incredible adult faith formation experience alongside the candidates as they prepare for Confirmation.

As you work through the program, ask yourself: How many Catholics do I know who would benefit from this program?

In time we hope that whole parishes will go through the Confirmation preparation experience together via the online, app, or e-mail versions of DECISION POINT.

"PEOPLE DON'T CARE HOW MUCH YOU KNOW, until they know HOW MUCH YOU CARE"

Theodore Roosevelt

GETTING STARTED

Leading a Confirmation class can be overwhelming. Teens can be daunting. But never forget that this is one of the most important things you will do in your life. These young people are hungry to make sense of life—and nothing does that like the Gospel.

We are going to spend a lot of time exploring incredible content, but interestingly the most important part of your role can be completely covered in one sentence—eight words, actually:

Make sure they know you care about them.

Theodore Roosevelt, the twenty-sixth president of the United States, perfectly summed up the scenario you are about to find yourself in when he wrote, **"People don't care how much you know, until they know how much you care."**

Start praying for the teens in your class today. Make an effort to know their names. Let them know you are praying for them every day. Pay attention to what is happening in their lives; they will reveal this to you in a hundred ways throughout your time together.

It's also important to realize that you cannot cover everything. You can't teach them everything about the Catholic faith. You can't combat every misconception they have about Catholicism. But if you give them a glimpse of the truth, beauty, and goodness that are at the core of our faith, they will get in touch with their appetite for these things—and that is no small thing. We have set you up with ideas and questions that will intrigue them and show them that Catholicism makes sense, that it works, that it is practical and joy filled, and that it is something that deep down they need and want. And remember, you don't have to have all the answers. If you don't know something, just say, "Good question. I don't know. Let's find out together."

When young people have questions about the faith, the questions are beautiful, because they represent their deepest yearnings. It doesn't matter how aggressively or disrespectfully the questions are asked. Never forget that every question comes from a yearning to know, love, and serve God. Young people may come at it in a very roundabout way, but don't we all?

Most of all, never get discouraged, and don't let what you can't do interfere with what you can do. What you can do is love these teens, walk with them in their journey, pray that they open themselves up to God's dream for their lives, and give them the most dynamic experience of Catholicism they have ever had.

13 Helpful Hints

FROM GREAT LEADERS

1. Greet your candidates at the door when they arrive for each class. Welcome them. Look them in the eye and thank them for coming.

2. Learn your candidates' names. This is the simplest way to demonstrate that they matter to you.

3. Start on time and end on time. Honoring time, honors people.

4. Speak up! Your voice is one of your best teaching tools. Be careful not to mumble or speak too quickly. A clear, slightly louder than normal voice is needed to lead a group. Say it like you mean it! You don't need to shout, but a firm voice says you're ready to lead.

5. Repeat yourself. Once is not enough. They need to hear important points over and over again. Make connections between what they learned and discussed last time you were together and what they are learning today. Keep repeating key phrases and themes. Repetition is a powerful force in educating and inspiring.

6. Look up! Whether they are sitting in a circle or in rows, make sure when you are speaking to look around the room. One temptation in leading a group is to speak only to those who are closest to you. Each class, make a conscious effort to make eye contact with everyone in the room.

7. Be prepared. Review the materials before class, mark the Scripture passages in your Bible, watch the videos, and ask the Holy Spirit to guide you. Being prepared sends so many messages to these young people: "You matter." "This is important." "I want to make this a great experience for you."

8. Tell your candidates what's up. Leading a group means guiding them step by step through the time together. So let them know what's next. "Now we are going to pray." The more specific the better. Feel free to add to your directions: "Now we are going to pray. Please bow your heads and close your eyes." Being specific helps our brains to envision directions. Putting directions in the positive—"Keep your glass up"—helps us get it right. When we put them in the negative—"Don't spill that"—we envision spilling the glass and often do just that!

9   Don't be afraid of silence. After you ask someone a question, anticipate a pause of several seconds. Some people need longer than others to process. That's OK. You can always go back to someone who needs more time. "I can see that you are working on your answer. I'll give you a moment." OR "Would you like me to come back to you?"

10   Redirect behavior. Tell them to cut it out. If you find yourself yelling, you are losing control of the group. Being prepared on the front end will help you lead well, without yelling. Being specific lets them know what is needed. A firm voice, not angry, sets the tone. "We are not talking right now. We are listening." "I am waiting on everyone to close their eyes to begin." (Make sure you look at them when you have to redirect.) You can turn this to the positive as well. This should be the voice of an appreciative, encouraging leader: "I really appreciate the way this group is working together on the activity. You are all listening to each other and sharing your ideas. Well done." Last, standing up and stretching is a great redirection. Sometimes we all just need to move. So move. If you move, lead this activity too. "Everyone up and let's stretch our legs." You may want to encourage them to trade seats. Moving is a helpful way to redirect behavior.

11   Smile. Really. Smiling at someone is a gift and conveys a sincere warmth. It just feels good when someone smiles at you.

12   Tell your story. One of the most powerful tools you have to lead this group is your story. Know your story and share it—not necessarily all at once, but in bits and pieces as they relate to the content. To successfully lead, you have to see your candidates as real people and they have to see you as a real person, and as crazy as that may sound, getting to this place can be harder than you think.

13   Be you. If you like sports trivia, use that as an icebreaker. If you love chocolate, give candy for prizes. If you love music, play some as they enter or as a closer. Let them get to know you.

THE CATHOLIC CHURCH is the biggest family in the WORLD

THE EXPERIENCE

DECISION POINT is a Dynamic Catholic program designed to prepare young Catholics for the Sacrament of Confirmation. The various components of the program can be experienced online or in the traditional format of workbook, leader guide, and DVDs.

At the heart of the program are seventy-two short films, which range in length from three to fifteen minutes and feature Matthew Kelly.

Here is a quick look at the different ways DECISION POINT can be experienced:

- **Online:** The entire program will be available online to anyone at any time.

- **Hard copies:** The workbook, leader guide, and DVD series will also be available as hard copies for parishes and individuals who prefer them.

- **E-mail:** The program will also be available in an e-mail version, which will allow individuals to sign up and receive the program in bite-size portions each week. Perfect for parents and sponsors.

- **App:** The seventy-two short films and bonus content will also be available on an application for smart phones and tablets.

- To learn more, visit **DynamicCatholic.com/Confirmation.**

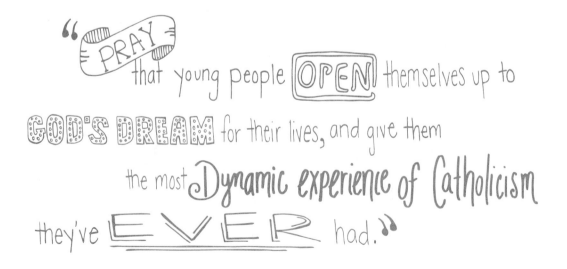

"PRAY that young people OPEN themselves up to GOD'S DREAM for their lives, and give them the most Dynamic experience of Catholicism they've EVER had."

#1 TIP

WE ARE COMMITTED TO HELPING YOU SUCCEED.

Every section has a little **TIP**.
These tips are usually just a sentence or two.

READ THROUGH ALL THE TIPS FROM START TO FINISH IN ONE SITTING. It will take you less than 30 minutes. This will give you a really good sense of how to engage these young Catholics in a dynamic experience. It will give you confidence. It will help you enjoy the process... and the more you enjoy it, the more they will enjoy it!

You are offering them something beautiful.
THEY NEED TO HEAR SOMETHING BEAUTIFUL, **TO EXPERIENCE SOMETHING BEAUTIFUL. THERE IS SO MUCH TRASH OUT** THERE AND THEY ARE ENCOUNTERING IT EVERY DAY.

GIVE THEM A *Beautiful* ENCOUNTER WITH GOD & HIS CHURCH AND YOU WILL CHANGE THEIR LIVES FOREVER.

You are about to change
THESE YOUNG PEOPLE'S LIVES.
DON'T LOSE SIGHT OF THAT.

THE FORMAT

One of the great challenges in developing Confirmation materials is that each diocese prepares candidates in different ways for different periods of time, with different class formats. With this in mind, DECISION POINT has been developed with a suggested format, but in a way that makes it infinitely flexible.

SUGGESTED FORMAT:

We suggest that the program be experienced through twelve one–hundred twenty minute classes. These can take place once a month for twelve months, twice a month for six months, or once a week for three months.

If this is not how you currently structure your Confirmation preparation, we invite you to consider trying something new. Just because you have always done it a certain way doesn't mean you need to continue to do it a certain way—especially if that way is not producing results.

But if your parish or diocese requires a different format, there are plenty of options.

OTHER FORMAT OPTIONS:

The core of the program is seventy-two short films. In the suggested format the candidates would experience six of these short films in each class. But you could use one per class for seventy-two sessions, or two per class for thirty-six sessions, or three per class for tweny-four sessions.

The program was specifically designed to have this flexibility. Each short film is content and concept rich. This leads to great opportunities for class or small group discussions.

There is also plenty of extra material and exercises in the workbook that are not used in the twelve-session format, for those parishes that have longer programs and need more material.

Life is
CHOICES

MY LORD GOD, I have no idea where I am going. I do not see the road ahead of me. I cannot know for certain where it will end. Nor do I really know myself... But I believe that the desire to please you does in fact please you. And I hope I have that desire in all that I am doing. Therefore I will trust you always though I may seem to be lost... I will not fear, for you are ever with me, and you will never leave me to face my perils alone.

— *Thomas Merton*

QUICK SESSION OVERVIEW

STEP 1	**WELCOME**
STEP 2	**OPENING PRAYER**
STEP 3	**ENGAGE – WATCH & DISCUSS**
STEP 4	**JOURNAL**
STEP 5	**ANNOUNCEMENTS**
STEP 6	**CLOSING PRAYER**

SESSION ONE: LIFE IS CHOICES

Objectives:

- To remind candidates that they make hundreds of choices every day and that every choice has consequences.

- To help candidates become better decision makers.

- To demonstrate that God's way and the way of the world are very different, and invite candidates to choose to walk with God.

STEP 1 WELCOME ·

From day one it is important to convey two things: that you care about the candidates and that you are excited.

Introduce yourself. Tell them a few things about you and your life—where you grew up, what football team you support, your hobbies, your favorite flavor of ice cream, and why you decided to be here with them right now.

Tell them this is going to be different from anything they have experienced before in a religious education class.

Take a few minutes and go around the class, asking each person to introduce him– or herself and share something just like you did.

Let them know you are praying for them. Encourage them to start praying for each other.

And remember what Theodore Roosevelt wrote: "People don't care how much you know, until they know how much you care."

LEADER GUIDE KEY

TIME-ICON: This icon serves as a guide to help you plan approximately how long each activity will take.

[WB5] This code serves as a reference to point you to the page in the Workbook where you can find the related activity/content.

Example: **[WB5]** *points you to page 5 in the Workbook*

The flag icon is the halfway mark and suggests a good breaking point if your program runs twenty-four classes (or approximately 60 minutes) instead of twelve 120 minute classes.

Tip

Get them quiet. Don't rush this. Begin with the sign of the cross. Make it with reverence; they are always watching you.

Allow them a moment of quiet before you start reading the prayer. You could say something like, "Let's just take a moment in silence to be still and quiet and open ourselves up to whatever God wants to lead us to today."

After thirty to forty seconds of silence—which will seem like an eternity for them, and maybe for you—read the prayer slowly and reflectively.

3 MIN

MY LORD GOD, I have no idea where I am going. I do not see the road ahead of me. I cannot know for certain where it will end. Nor do I really know myself... But I believe that the desire to please you does in fact please you. And I hope I have that desire in all that I am doing. Therefore I will trust you always though I may seem to be lost... I will not fear, for you are ever with me, and you will never leave me to face my perils alone.

·——————— *Thomas Merton* ———·

SESSION 1 INTRODUCTION

WATCH VIDEO

8 MIN

 TIP: This is the first short film they are going to experience in the program. Make sure everyone can see the screen. Encourage them to turn off their phones. You may want to consider establishing cell phone rules now. Otherwise they may become the bane of your existence.

DISCUSSION QUESTION

6 MIN

1) What is the one idea in this short film that you found most helpful?

Did you notice the kid in the film talking on his cell phone? Use this opportunity to talk to the class about how dangerous that can be.

SESSION 1.1 YOUR CHOICES MATTER

WATCH VIDEO

7 MIN

1.1 YOUR *choices* MATTER

DISCUSSION QUESTIONS [WB5]

10 MIN

Tip If your group is less than twenty people, you can have the discussion as a class. If you have more than that, you may want to consider breaking them up into small groups.

1) Who do you know who is a great decision maker? What makes this person a great decision maker?

2) Describe a time when you ignored your conscience and regretted it later. Describe a time when you listened to your conscience and followed it, even though it was difficult.

3) Are you good at making decisions? On a scale of 1 to 10 (10 being the best), how good do you think you are at making decisions? What's one practical thing you could do to become a better decision maker?

EXERCISE

5 MIN

Every session highlights a saint. Invite a student to read
"Who was Joan of Arc?" from the workbook.
Ask the class what else they know about her. [WB3]

TIP! Talk a little about how much courage Joan of Arc must have needed to do what she did. Then share about a time in your life when you needed courage to do something.

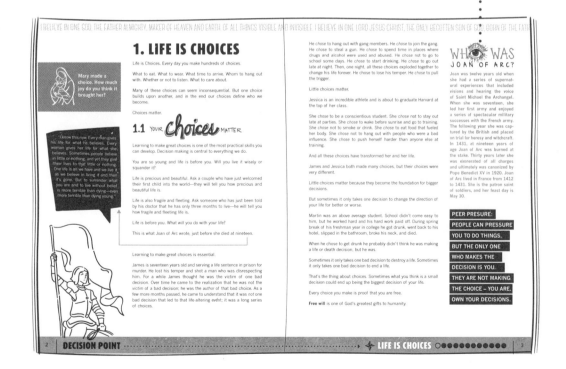

I BELIEVE IN ONE GOD, THE FATHER ALMIGHTY, MAKER OF HEAVEN AND EARTH, OF ALL THINGS VISIBLE AND INVISIBLE. I BELIEVE IN ONE LORD JESUS CHRIST, THE ONLY BEGOTTEN SON OF GOD, BORN OF THE FATH

1. LIFE IS CHOICES

Mary made a choice. How much joy do you think it brought her?

Life is Choices. Every day you make hundreds of choices.

What to eat. What to wear. What time to arrive. Whom to hang out with. Whether or not to listen. What to care about.

Many of these choices can seem inconsequential. But one choice builds upon another, and in the end our choices define who we become.

Choices matter.

"I know this now. Every man gives his life for what he believes. Every woman gives her life for what she believes. Sometimes people believe in little or nothing, and yet they give their lives to that little or nothing. One life is all we have and we live it as we believe in living it and then it's gone. But to surrender what you are and to live without belief is more terrible than dying—even more terrible than dying young."

1.1 YOUR *Choices* MATTER

Learning to make great choices is one of the most practical skills you can develop. Decision making is central to everything we do.

You are so young and life is before you. Will you live it wisely or squander it?

Life is precious and beautiful. Ask a couple who have just welcomed their first child into the world—they will tell you how precious and beautiful life is.

Life is also fragile and fleeting. Ask someone who has just been told by his doctor that he has only three months to live—he will tell you how fragile and fleeting life is.

Life is before you. What will you do with your life?

This is what Joan of Arc wrote, just before she died at nineteen.

Learning to make great choices is essential.

James is seventeen years old and serving a life sentence in prison for murder. He lost his temper and shot a man who was disrespecting him. For a while James thought he was the victim of one bad decision. Over time he came to the realization that he was not the victim of a bad decision; he was the author of that bad choice. As a few more months passed, he came to understand that it was not one bad decision that led to that life-altering event; it was a long series of choices.

He chose to hang out with gang members. He chose to join the gang. He chose to steal a gun. He chose to spend time in places where drugs and alcohol were used and abused. He chose not to go to school some days. He chose to start drinking. He chose to go out late at night. Then, one night, all these choices exploded together to change his life forever. He chose to lose his temper. He chose to pull the trigger.

Little choices matter.

Jessica is an incredible athlete and is about to graduate Harvard at the top of her class.

She chose to be a conscientious student. She chose not to stay out late at parties. She chose to wake before sunrise and go to training. She chose not to smoke or drink. She chose to eat food that fueled her body. She chose not to hang out with people who were a bad influence. She chose to push herself harder than anyone else at training.

And all these choices have transformed her and her life.

James and Jessica both made many choices, but their choices were very different.

Little choices matter because they become the foundation for bigger decisions.

But sometimes it only takes one decision to change the direction of your life for better or worse.

Martin was an above average student. School didn't come easy to him, but he worked hard and his hard work paid off. During spring break of his freshman year in college he got drunk, went back to his hotel, slipped in the bathroom, broke his neck, and died.

When he chose to get drunk he probably didn't think he was making a life or death decision, but he was.

Sometimes it only takes one bad decision to destroy a life. Sometimes it only takes one bad decision to end a life.

That's the thing about choices. Sometimes what you think is a small decision could end up being the biggest decision of your life.

Every choice you make is proof that you are free.

Free will is one of God's greatest gifts to humanity.

WHO WAS JOAN OF ARC?

Joan was twelve years old when she had a series of supernatural experiences that included visions and hearing the voice of Saint Michael the Archangel. When she was seventeen, she led her first army and enjoyed a series of spectacular military successes with the French army. The following year she was captured by the British and placed on trial for heresy and witchcraft. In 1431, at nineteen years of age Joan of Arc was burned at the stake. Thirty years later she was exonerated of all charges and ultimately was canonized by Pope Benedict XV in 1920. Joan of Arc lived in France from 1412 to 1431. She is the patron saint of soldiers, and her feast day is May 30.

**PEER PRESURE:
PEOPLE CAN PRESSURE
YOU TO DO THINGS,
BUT THE ONLY ONE
WHO MAKES THE
DECISION IS YOU.
THEY ARE NOT MAKING
THE CHOICE – YOU ARE.
OWN YOUR DECISIONS.**

2 | **DECISION POINT**

LIFE IS CHOICES ○●●●●●●●●●● | 3

SESSION 1.2 THE BEST WAY TO LIVE

WATCH VIDEO

6 MIN

1.2 the BEST way to live

If you had a chance to watch this short film before class, tell the students about your favorite part. Not too much—just enough to arouse curiosity. This will help them to focus, waiting for the part you mentioned.

10 MIN

DISCUSSION QUESTIONS [WB11]

1) In some ways the best way to live is the same for us all. Which of the three principles had the most impact on you (the-best-version-of-yourself, virtue, or self-control)?

2) How would your relationships improve if you started to really live these three principles?

3) If at the end of your life you could be remembered for just one virtue, which would you choose? Why is that virtue important to you?

SESSION 1.3 GOD'S DREAM FOR YOU

WATCH VIDEO

7 MIN

TIP

Don't rush it. Don't be constantly looking at the clock. If you do, they will. If you don't finish everything, that's OK! Hopefully that means you have been having some great discussions. Discussion = Engagement. If you don't get through the whole session, ask them to watch the remaining videos on the app and to journal about the discussion questions in their workbooks at home.

DISCUSSION QUESTIONS [WB17]

10 MIN

1) Have you ever met someone and discovered that person was nothing like what you thought he or she would be like?

2) Who in your life is helping you become the-best-version-of-yourself?

3) What are two things you can do to become a-better-version-of-yourself this week?

5 MIN

EXERCISE: WHAT'S ENSLAVING YOU?

Tip

Ask your class to fill out the diagram on page 18 of their workbooks. If you want them to make themselves vulnerable to the process, you need to make yourself vulnerable to them first. Share with the class what is enslaving you at the moment or what has enslaved you in the past.

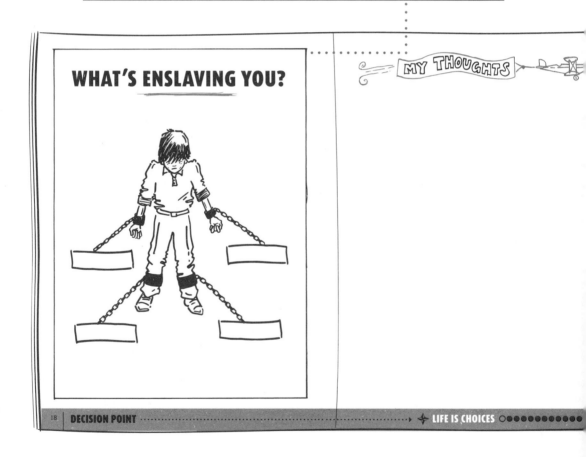

MY THOUGHTS

WHAT'S ENSLAVING YOU?

18 | DECISION POINT ·································· → ✦ LIFE IS CHOICES ○●●●●●●●●●●

SESSION 1.4 BE A REBEL

WATCH VIDEO

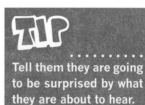

Tell them they are going to be surprised by what they are about to hear.

5 MIN

DISCUSSION QUESTIONS [WB22]

10 MIN

1) When was the last time you watched something on TV that helped you become a-better-version-of-yourself?

2) In what ways do you feel called to rebel against today's culture?

3) How is the path God is calling you along different and better than the culture's way of doing things?

EXERCISE — VIRTUE IN FOCUS

🕐 5 MIN

TIP

Every session highlights a virtue. Invite a student to read the **Virtue in Focus** section. Choose one of the questions from the section and ask students to share their answers. [WB21]

AIN IN GLORY TO JUDGE THE LIVING AND THE DEAD AND HIS KINGDOM WILL HAVE NO END. I BELIEVE IN THE HOLY SPIRIT, THE LORD, THE GIVER OF LIFE, WHO PROCEEDS FROM THE FATHER AND

ho Was ——— OSES? 1.4 be a REBEL

orn when his people sing in numbers ptian Pharaoh was fear them. Moses' him when Pharaoh at all newborn be killed. The boy nd adopted by the yal family. After yptian slave master, cross the Red Sea, ountered God in the n. God sent Moses Pharaoh to set the e. After God sent o convince Pharaoh e Israelites, Moses odus out of Egypt he Red Sea toward - where he received mmandments. But r made it to the nd. He died within after wandering in r forty years. Moses er! But look what he accomplish after he to God.

MOSES

It's probably the last thing that you expected to hear at church, but I really want to encourage you to be a rebel. Jesus was a rebel.

But here's the thing: It's important to rebel against the right things.

Today's culture doesn't want you to become the-best-version-of-yourself. Today's culture doesn't want you to think too much about life. Today's culture doesn't want you to become hungry for the truth. Today's culture doesn't want you to develop your spiritual self. Today's culture doesn't want you to have a great relationship with God.

Modern culture just wants you to go along, be a good, obedient little consumer, and not ask too many questions about where the whole experiment is leading.

I want you to rebel against that. I want you to rebel against the modern culture.

Now, let's compare God's vision for you and your life with the modern culture's vision for you and your life.

God loves you deeply and wants you to become the-best-version-of-yourself. The culture doesn't care about you and usually leads you toward a-second-rate-version-of-yourself.

What drives God? Love. What's driving the culture? Consumption.

Almost everything that happens in today's culture is aimed at getting you to buy something, or feel inadequate, or both.

Everything has a brand on it today. What did we first use brands on? That's right: cattle. What did we next use brands on? Correct again: slaves. Do we own the brands or do the brands own us? Are we still the consumers or are we being consumed? We need to start thinking at a deeper level. Are we cattle and slaves or free men and women?

God sees us as his children. He created us *free* and wants to keep us free. The culture sees us as cattle and wants to turn us into slaves.

Do you want to be a child of God or a slave to the culture?

The problem is most of us spend a lot more time listening to the culture than we do listening to God.

It's time to rebel.

Reject the world's vision for your life, because it leads to emptiness and misery, in this life and the next life. *Embrace* and celebrate God's vision for your life, because it leads to joy and fullness, now and forever.

They say that every teenager goes through a rebellious stage. But we usually rebel against the wrong things. If you want to rebel against something, rebel against the culture that wants to rob you of your best self and enslave you. Rebel against the things that seek to make you less than who you really are.

The history of our great faith is full of examples of men and women who rejected the culture's vision for their life.

Anthony of the Desert inherited an enormous fortune as a young man when his parents died. The vision the culture had for him was to live a life of privilege and luxury as a wealthy landowner. He rejected the culture's vision for his life when he heard the words of Jesus: *"If you want to be perfect, go, sell what you possess and give to the poor, and you will have treasures in heaven; and come, and follow me."* (Matthew 19:21) Anthony sold or gave away all his land and possessions, gave the money for the care of the poor, and became a hermit. Over time he developed the monastic way of life, and he is now considered the father of all monks.

Now, this story may seem far from the world you live in. But reconsider it. Was Anthony's decision a difficult one? Yes. Was it a courageous decision? Yes. Did many of his friends think he was crazy? Yes. Did he have to overcome his own selfish desires? Yes.

Your world is not that different. When you decide to walk with God you will have to make tough choices, courageous decisions. Many of your friends will think you are crazy, and you too will need to overcome your selfish desires.

You and Anthony are not that different.

Reject the modern culture and the world's empty vision for your life. Embrace God. You will be happier.

What do you think Mary's friends said about her?

VIRTUE IN 👓 FOCUS

pa·tience
[pey-shuh ns]

The capacity to accept or tolerate delay, trouble, or suffering without getting angry or upset.

Who is the most patient person you know?

How do they practice patience?

What are three ways you can become a more patient person?

MATTHEW 19:21

KNOW IT: The things of this world are fleeting and worthless compared to the treasures of the next world.

THINK ABOUT IT: If Jesus asked you to give up everything and follow him, what would be the hardest thing to give up?

LIVE IT: Go without something this week.

ION POINT ➡ **LIFE IS CHOICES** ⬤⬤⬤⬤⬤⬤⬤⬤⬤⬤⬤ 21

SESSION 1.5 DECISION POINT

WATCH VIDEO

2 MIN

> **Tip**
>
> Let them know that this is a really short but important film.

EXERCISE: Know It. Think About It. Live It.

5 MIN

TIP

Encourage them to bring a Bible to class. Throughout the program we will highlight verses from the Bible in exactly the same way: **KNOW IT. THINK ABOUT IT. LIVE IT.** We will only explore one of these verses together, but each time you do, encourage them to open their Bibles and find the passage. Getting young people comfortable with a Bible in their hands is another huge leap in their spiritual journey. [WB24]

WHO PROCEEDS FROM THE FATHER AND THE SON WHO WITH THE FATHER AND THE SON IS ADORED AND

"DO NOT BE AFRAID."
—JESUS CHRIST

1.5 DECISION point

One of the great figures in the Bible is Moses. He led the Israelites out of slavery in Egypt and toward the Promised Land.

When Moses was about to die he said to Joshua and the people of Israel, "I have set before you today life and prosperity, death and adversity." (Deuteronomy 30:15)

DEUTERONOMY 30:15

KNOW IT: Joshua is telling the Israelites: You are at a Decision Point.

THINK ABOUT IT: Are you choosing life or death, prosperity or adversity in your daily decisions?

LIVE IT: When you are deciding what to eat this week, choose life and prosperity.

JOHN 10:10

KNOW IT: God wants good things for you! Jesus wants to help you live life to the fullest!

THINK ABOUT IT: If you were living life to the fullest, how would your life be different?

LIVE IT: Do one thing today that will help you live the incredible life God has imagined for you.

What was Moses saying to the people? You choose--life or death. You choose--prosperity or adversity.

Throughout our journey together you are going to face many decision points. They matter. They may not seem like life or death decisions, but they are.

Jesus said, "I have come so that you may have life, and have it to the fullest." (John 10:10.)

Do you want to live life to the fullest? God will not force fullness of life on you. God has given you free will and he will let you use that free will to live a shallow and empty life if that is what you choose. What do you choose?

I have placed before you today God's incredible vision for your life and the world's empty vision for your life. Which do you choose?

The best version of yourself or some second-rate version of yourself?

Freedom or slavery?

DEATH — LIFE
ADVERSITY — PROSPERITY

JOURNAL
QUESTIONS

1. DO YOU WANT TO LIVE LIFE TO THE FULLEST? WHY OR WHY NOT?

2. ARE YOU GOING TO CHOOSE GOD'S INCREDIBLE VISION FOR YOUR LIFE OR THE WORLD'S EMPTY VISION FOR YOUR LIFE?

3. WHAT IS ONE MESSAGE FROM THIS SESSION THAT YOU ARE GOING TO SHARE WITH SOMEONE ELSE?

STEP 4 JOURNAL

8 MIN

INSTRUCTIONS: Invite your class to open up to page 25 and take a few minutes in silence to journal their answers to those questions.

TIP

Getting people to start listening to the voice of God is a huge step. Once they are tuned in to God's radio station, he can communicate with them constantly and lead them in the paths he has designed just for them.

STEP 5 ANNOUNCEMENTS

3 MIN

Tip

Thank them for coming. Seriously. Thank them. And thank them for participating, even if they didn't participate as you would have liked them to. Praise and encouragement brings the best out of us all. Remind them you will be praying for them. You might say something like, "Remember, if you have a tough week or find yourself in a difficult situation, I am praying for you." Encourage them to watch the videos again for homework online or on the app—and to journal.

STEP 6 CLOSING PRAYER

TIP

The closing prayer for every session is a Psalm. Why a Psalm? We are trying to immerse these young Catholics in the life of the Church in a thousand ways, most of which they will not realize are happening. Read it slowly. After the Psalm you may want to finish with a spontaneous prayer asking God to bless and guide you and the students in the coming week.

5 MIN

Psalm 1: The Two Ways

[1] Blessed is the man who walks not in the counsel of the wicked, nor stands in the way of sinners, nor sits in the seat of scoffers;

[2] but his delight is in the law of the Lord, and on his law he meditates day and night.

[3] He is like a tree planted by streams of water, that yields its fruit in its season, and its leaf does not wither. In all that he does, he prospers.

[4] The wicked are not so, but are like chaff which the wind drives away.

[5] Therefore the wicked will not stand in the judgment, nor sinners in the congregation of the righteous;

[6] for the Lord knows the way of the righteous, but the way of the wicked will perish.

SESSION TWO

What's ——————

HOLDING

————— *you back?*

O Lord my God, teach my heart this day where and how to see you, where and how to find you. You have made me and remade me, and you have bestowed on me all the good things I possess, and still I do not know you. I have not yet done that for which I was made. Teach me to seek you, for I cannot seek you unless you teach me, or find you unless you show yourself to me. Let me seek you in my desire, let me desire you in my seeking. Let me find you by loving you, let me love you when I find you. Amen.

St. Anselm

QUICK SESSION OVERVIEW

STEP 1 WELCOME

STEP 2 OPENING PRAYER

STEP 3 ENGAGE – WATCH & DISCUSS

STEP 4 JOURNAL

STEP 5 ANNOUNCEMENTS

STEP 6 CLOSING PRAYER

SESSION TWO: WHAT'S HOLDING YOU BACK?

Objectives:

- To demonstrate that all paths are not equal and that there is such a thing as objective truth.

- To teach candidates to recognize patterns of stinking thinking in their lives.

- To help candidates to recognize who and what is holding them back from living the incredible life God invites them to.

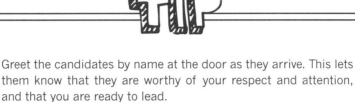

Greet the candidates by name at the door as they arrive. This lets them know that they are worthy of your respect and attention, and that you are ready to lead.

LEADER GUIDE KEY

TIME-ICON: This icon serves as a guide to help you plan approximately how long each activity will take.

[WB5] This code serves as a reference to point you to the page in the Workbook where you can find the related activity/content.

Example: **[WB5]** *points you to page 5 in the Workbook*

The flag icon is the halfway mark and suggests a good breaking point if your program runs twenty-four classes (or approximately 60 minutes) instead of twelve 120 minute classes.

Tip

Take a moment to get them quiet.

Now, speak to them about why quiet time is important in your life. The more specific you can be, the more they will latch on to this habit. How does quiet time make you a better person, friend, husband, wife, father, mother?

Begin with the Sign of the Cross, invite them to close their eyes, and read the opening prayer slowly and deliberately. Then give them thirty seconds in silence to reflect on the prayer and what God is saying to them through it.

4 MIN

O Lord my God, teach my heart this day where and how to see you, where and how to find you. You have made me and remade me, and you have bestowed on me all the good things I possess, and still I do not know you. I have not yet done that for which I was made. Teach me to seek you, for I cannot seek you unless you teach me, or find you unless you show yourself to me. Let me seek you in my desire, let me desire you in my seeking. Let me find you by loving you, let me love you when I find you. Amen.

·——— *St. Anselm* ———·

STEP 3 ENGAGE: WATCH & DISCUSS

SESSION 2 INTRODUCTION

WATCH VIDEO

4 MIN

TIP: Make sure you are paying attention. Even if you have watched the short film ten times to prepare for class, watch it like it is the first time you are seeing it.

DISCUSSION QUESTION

6 MIN

1) What is the one idea in this short film that you found most helpful?

SESSION 2.1 **THE QUEST FOR HAPPINESS**

WATCH VIDEO

8 MIN

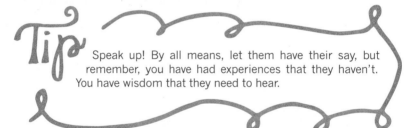

2.1 THE *Quest* FOR HAPPINESS

DISCUSSION QUESTIONS [WB34]

10 MIN

Tip Speak up! By all means, let them have their say, but remember, you have had experiences that they haven't. You have wisdom that they need to hear.

1) What are some things you desire that are good for you?

2) What is something you thought would make you happy, but in fact left you feeling empty, unhappy, miserable, used, deceived, or worse?

3) Describe a time when you had the wisdom and courage to follow your conscience, and you were glad you did.

EXERCISE

Every session highlights a saint or biblical figure. Invite a student to read **"Who Was Mother Teresa?"** from the workbook. Ask the class what else they know about her or what they admire about her. [WB32]

5 MIN

TIP! Sometimes young people can be slow to participate, so it might be helpful if you are ready to share how Mother Teresa inspires you.

I CONFESS ONE BAPTISM FOR THE FORGIVENESS OF SINS AND I LOOK FORWARD TO THE RESURRECTION OF THE DEAD AND THE LIFE OF THE WORLD TO COME. AMEN. I BELIEVE IN ONE GOD, THE FATHER ALMIGHTY

WHO WAS

Mother Teresa?

Mother Teresa (1910–1997) founded the Missionaries of Charity, a religious congregation made up of more than forty-five hundred religious sisters who are active in 133 countries. Their work consists of running homes and hospice facilities for those with HIV/AIDS, leprosy, and tuberculosis; soup kitchens; orphanages; family counseling programs; and schools. Members of the order take four vows: the traditional vows of poverty, chastity, and obedience, and a fourth vow, "To give wholehearted and free service to the poorest of the poor." Mother Teresa had an immense love for the unloved. "We think sometimes that poverty is only being hungry, naked, and homeless. The poverty of being unwanted, unloved and uncared for is the greatest poverty. We must start in our own homes to remedy this kind of poverty."

Happiness is different. Happiness is sustainable.

Here's another example. I come home from work one day next week, and it is my day to work out, but I don't really feel like working out. So I have to make a decision: Work out or plant myself in a recliner in front of my 127-inch idiot box with a six-pack of beer and a three-hundred-ounce bag of potato chips?

The choice is mine.

Now, suppose I force myself to work out even though I don't feel like it. The thing is, whenever I get done working out I am always glad—even if I had to force myself to do it. Happiness can be sustained beyond the activity producing it.

Happiness is more than pleasure. *Don't settle for an empty life of pleasure.* Choose more. Rebel against the culture of pleasure and start actively seeking the happiness God created you for.

So, what will really make you happy?

Happiness is the result of **right living**. Honesty leads to happiness; dishonesty leads to misery. Caring for others leads to happiness; selfishness leads to unhappiness. Patience leads to happiness; impatience will make you miserable.

There are right and wrong ways to live your life. The culture tells us that there is no right and wrong. The culture says that what's wrong for you might be right for me. This is nonsense. Hitler's way was wrong. Mother Teresa's way was right.

But how do you know what is the *right* thing to do?

At a basic level, you just know. One of God's great gifts to you is **conscience**. Your conscience guides you in the way of right living so that you can celebrate the-best-version-of-yourself, and live your best life.

Very often we say we don't know what we should do, but we are lying to ourselves (and to others), because our conscience is telling us the right course of action but we are trying to ignore it.

Our regrets are born when we ignore our conscience.

But there may be a handful of times in your life when you legitimately don't know what the right thing to do is. It is for these times more than any other that God has given you another of his great gifts: **reason**.

I had dinner last week with some friends, Mike and Samantha. They have been married for two years and have been trying to have a baby,

but have not become pregnant. Their friends have been telling them about different types of fertility treatments, but they don't know if these treatments are part of God's dream for them. Mike and Jessica want to do the right thing, but they are not sure what the right thing to do is. This is a highly specialized and complex area of science and morality. To get to the truth they are going to need to study this issue.

This is a perfect example of why God gave you a *beautiful mind*. You have the ability to study an issue, search for the truth, think things through, seek out God's way, and act on the truth you discover.

If you want to make great decisions, *just do the next right thing*. Don't worry about what you have to do next week or next year; just do the next right thing right now.

Five, ten, fifty, one hundred times a day. Do the next right thing often enough and you will live a life uncommon, a life that is rich with inner peace and happiness.

THE TRUTH WILL SET YOU free JOHN 8:32

WHO WAS Hitler?

Adolf Hitler (1889–1945) was the leader of the Nazi Party and Chancellor of Germany from 1933 to 1945. Hitler's was the diabolical mind behind the Holocaust; his regime was responsible for the deaths of six million Jews, as well as millions of others he and his followers considered racially or genetically inferior.

JOHN 8:32

KNOW IT: God created you for freedom and wants you to be free. Jesus is telling us that truth is essential for freedom and happiness.

THINK ABOUT IT: What lies are enslaving you?

LIVE IT: Make a conscious effort to align your actions with the truth this week.

SESSION 2.2 **STINKING THINKING**

WATCH VIDEO

4 MIN

2.2 STINKING THINKING

▶

TIP Introduce the video. "The next video is about stinking thinking. After the video I will tell you about a time in my life when I fell into stinking thinking."

DISCUSSION QUESTIONS [WB38]

10 MIN

1) How is "Stinking Thinking" holding you back from becoming the person God created you to be?

2) Individualism, hedonism, minimalism, relativism: which of these are the biggest temptations for you at this time in your life?

3) Describe a time when you embraced one of these broken philosophies. What was the outcome? How did you feel afterward? Did you become a-better-version-of-yourself?

SESSION 2.3 HUNGRY FOR THE TRUTH

WATCH VIDEO

4 MIN

TIP

Don't be afraid of silence. After you ask someone a question, be prepared for a pause of several seconds. Some people need longer than others to process. That's OK. You can always go back to someone who needs more time. After several seconds, if you sense he or she still needs a little more time, ask, "Would you like me to come back to you?"

DISCUSSION QUESTIONS [WB42]

10 MIN

1) Describe a time when you were not "hungry for truth," when you didn't want to know the truth. Why were you avoiding it?

2) Think about a disturbing story you have seen in the news recently. What happened? Which of the Ten Commandments were broken?

3) When we examine the Ten Commandments, the obvious ways of violating them are apparent, but what are some of the more subtle ways we can break them? For example, most people will never be in a situation in which they are tempted to break the Fifth Commandment (You shall not kill). But most of us have killed someone's reputation with gossip. Go through the commandments one by one and discuss the not-so-obvious ways each can be broken.

5 MIN

EXERCISE: THE TEN COMMANDMENTS

Work through the Ten Commandments and discuss the less obvious ways we can break them. For example, the Fifth Commandment is "You shall not kill." Most of us wouldn't think of killing another person physically, but it is easy to kill a person's reputation with gossip and lies. [WB41]

Tip

Learn to keep control of the conversation. Don't be afraid to tell them to cut it out. You are the leader, and part of your job is to redirect behavior.

...VE IN ONE LORD JESUS CHRIST, THE ONLY BEGOTTEN SON OF GOD, BORN OF THE FATHER BEFORE ALL AGES, GOD FROM GOD, LIGHT FROM LIGHT, TRUE GOD FROM TRUE GOD, BEGOTTEN, NOT MADE, CONSUBS...

WHAT IS WISDOM?

Wisdom is not the amassing of knowledge. The sheer volume of information available on the Internet is enough to boggle the mind, and experts say the amount of data will soon double every day. But information is not **wisdom**. In fact, even if you could commit all this information to memory and claim it as knowledge, knowledge is not **wisdom**. So, what is **wisdom**? **Wisdom** is truth lived.

TRUTH & HAPPINESS ARE CONNECTED

2.3 HUNGRY FOR THE TRUTH

One of the beautiful things about young people is *you are hungry for the truth*. And because of this hunger for the truth, you *hate being lied to*.

The broken philosophies we just explored and the stinking thinking that comes with them lead to the lie that there is no truth—and if there is no truth, there is no right and wrong. This is among the most absurd claims modern culture makes.

This kind of stinking thinking makes happiness impossible.

The good news is *there is truth*. Some things are true for everybody. There is such a thing as right and wrong.

You know this already from your own experience. Tell a lie and you will feel uncomfortable with yourself. You will also notice that lying makes you more anxious and less joyful. Anxiety represents the world. Joy represents God. Every lie takes you further away from God and his joy, and deeper into the anxiousness of the world.

If someone else lies to you, you feel that they have wronged you in some way. How can they wrong you if there is no right and wrong?

You're smarter than the culture. Rebel against it.

There is such a thing as truth—not this rubbish of *your truth and my truth*, but **universal truth**. Truth is bigger than you and me; truth is bigger than everyone. There is such a thing as right and wrong. And you will only ever be happy to the extent that you align your life with truth, and make choices based upon what is right.

Truth and happiness are connected.

Ever since Adam and Eve were in the Garden of Eden, God has been trying to lead us in this truth, and we have been rebelling. When we walk with God in his truth we find happiness and fulfillment. When we rebel against God and turn our backs on his truth, we find misery and discontent.

THE WORLD'S WAY / FOLLOW JESUS

In the book of Exodus we read the story of Moses leading the people out of slavery in Egypt and into the Promised Land. Every person and every culture has questions about what is right and wrong. This is how God answered the Israelites' questions:

1. You shall love the Lord your God and serve him only.
2. You shall not take the name of the Lord your God in vain.
3. Keep holy the Sabbath.
4. Honor your father and your mother.
5. You shall not kill.
6. You shall not commit adultery.
7. You shall not steal.
8. You shall not bear false witness.
9. You shall not covet your neighbor's wife.
10. You shall not covet your neighbor's goods.

I know, it may seem a little old-fashioned, but *wisdom is never old-fashioned*. Let me suggest an exercise. Watch the news tomorrow night with this list in front of you. As each story is presented you will notice that most of the news is bad news. (The culture focuses on what is bad. God invites you to focus on what is good.) After each story is presented in the news program, ask yourself, which of the Ten Commandments was broken?

The truth is, the list is brilliant. It is pure genius. Wherever you find injustice and misery in this world, you will discover that at least one of the Ten Commandments has been broken.

Now ask yourself: How would the world be different if we just lived by the Ten Commandments?

Imagine all the misery and heartache that could be avoided if we all just lived by these ten nuggets of life-giving wisdom.

What do you think was Mary's favorite Scripture passage?

the Book of EXODUS

The Book of Exodus is the second book in the Old Testament. It tells the story of how the people of Israel, led by Moses, left slavery in Egypt. They journeyed through the wilderness to Mount Sinai, where God promised them the land of Canaan ("the Promised Land") in return for their faithfulness. Israel entered into a covenant with God, who gave them laws to live by and instructions for the Tabernacle. It was in the Tabernacle that God promised to live among them, lead them to the Promised Land, and give them peace.

I
You shall love the Lord your God and serve Him only.

II
You shall not take the name of the Lord God in vain.

III
Keep Holy the Sabbath.

VI
Honor your father and mother.

VII
You shall not kill.

VIII
You shall not commit adultery.

IX
You shall not steal.

IV
You shall not bear false witness.

You shall not covet your neighbor's wife.

DECISION POINT → 🔒 **WHAT'S HOLDING YOU BACK?** ○○●●●●●●●●●● 41

SESSION 2.4 **THIS IS PERSONAL**

WATCH VIDEO

 . . . .

Tell them they are about to hear an incredibly powerful story.

 7 MIN

DISCUSSION QUESTIONS [WB47]

10 MIN

1) What did the story about the rattlesnake make you think?

2) What does the rattlesnake represent for you? Who or what is holding you back? What is it that sooner or later is going to turn on you and strike you down? How would your life be better if you could walk away from that rattlesnake?

3) If you had more courage, what good thing would you do?

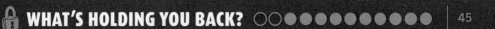

EXERCISE VIRTUE IN FOCUS

TIP

5 MIN

Every session highlights a virtue. Invite a candidate to read the **Virtue in Focus** section. Choose one of the questions from the section and ask the candidates to share their answers. [WB37]

THE FATHER ALMIGHTY, MAKER OF HEAVEN AND EARTH, OF ALL THINGS VISIBLE AND INVISIBLE. I BELIEVE IN ONE LORD JESUS CHRIST, THE ONLY BEGOTTEN SON OF GOD, BORN OF THE FATH

2.2 Stinking Thinking

Even though God has given us incredible minds to reason with, we still do a lot of **stinking thinking**. Let's take a quick look at some of the paths that the world proposes for happiness.

Individualism. The creed of the individualist is: What's in it for me? Individualism is the philosophy of selfishness. The fruits of individualism are greed, selfishness, isolation, and exploitation.

Individualism is stinking thinking.

Hedonism. The creed of the hedonist is: Pleasure is the ultimate goal in life; if it feels good, do it! The fruits of hedonism are laziness, gluttony, procrastination, and lust.

Hedonism is stinking thinking.

Minimalism. The creed of the minimalist is: What's the least I can do? A minimalist is always seeking to exert the minimum effort and receive the maximum reward. Minimalism is the enemy of excellence and the father of mediocrity.

Minimalism is stinking thinking.

Relativism. The creed of the Relativist is: There is no absolute truth; what's true for you may not be true for me! Relativism contradicts itself because it claims, "It is absolutely true for everybody that nothing is absolutely true for everybody." The fruits of relativism are disorientation, intellectual and spiritual confusion, and hopelessness caused by the loss of any meaning in life.

Relativism is stinking thinking.

Great thoughts are beautiful. Great actions are inspiring. Are any of these philosophies beautiful? I think not. When someone embraces these broken ways of thinking and living, do they inspire anything good? Absolutely not.

They may be convenient to your disordered desires and selfishness at a particular moment, but do they really suffice as a philosophy to live your life by?

Reject the world's vision for your life. *It will leave you empty and dissatisfied.* Rebel against the culture.

Reject these broken philosophies and watch out for people who live by them, because they will only use you for their own benefit and selfish gratification.

Beyond yourself, these philosophies also mean doom for communities of any size.

What would happen to a community—a family, a parish, or a nation—if everyone lived by these self-centered philosophies? Those communities would grow apart, fall apart, and self-destruct.

In many ways this is what we are witnessing in world affairs today. As modern cultures and nations become increasingly secular, rejecting God and his ways, they begin to implode. *Anything that stands against God and his truth cannot last.*

Truth, beauty, and goodness: These are what your soul is thirsty for. The philosophies the world wants to pass off to you are deficient in all three.

VIRTUE IN FOCUS

Cour·age
[kur·ij]

Mental or moral strength to venture, persevere, and withstand danger, fear, or difficulty.

What has been the most courageous moment of your life?

Who is the most courageous person you know?

In what situations would you like to have more courage?

SESSION 2.5 DECISION POINT

WATCH VIDEO

2.5 DECISION point

> **Tip**
> Compliment them. We all shine when we realize that someone cares enough to notice.

3 MIN

EXERCISE: Know It. Think About It. Live It.

Keep encouraging them to bring a Bible to class. Bring some extra Bibles if you have any. Each time, invite a different student to find the passage in the Bible and read it to the class. [WB33]

TIP

5 MIN

I CONFESS ONE BAPTISM FOR THE FORGIVENESS OF SINS AND I LOOK FORWARD TO THE RESURRECTION OF THE DEAD AND THE LIFE OF THE WORLD TO COME. AMEN. I BELIEVE IN ONE GOD, THE FATHER ALMIGHTY,

WHO WAS Mother Teresa?

Mother Teresa (1910-1997) founded the Missionaries of Charity, a religious congregation made up of more than forty-five hundred religious sisters who are active in 133 countries. Their work consists of running homes and hospice facilities for those with HIV/AIDS, leprosy, and tuberculosis; soup kitchens; orphanages; family counseling programs; and schools. Members of the order take four vows: the traditional vows of poverty, chastity, and obedience, and a fourth vow, "To give wholehearted and free service to the poorest of the poor." Mother Teresa had an immense love for the unloved: "We think sometimes that poverty is only being hungry, naked, and homeless. The poverty of being unwanted, unloved and uncared for is the greatest poverty. We must start in our own homes to remedy this kind of poverty."

Happiness is different. Happiness is sustainable.

Here's another example. I come home from work one day next week, and it is my day to work out, but I don't really feel like working out. So I have to make a decision: Work out or plant myself in a recliner in front of my 127-inch idiot box with a six-pack of beer and a three-hundred-ounce bag of potato chips?

The choice is mine.

Now, suppose I force myself to work out even though I don't feel like it. The thing is, whenever I get done working out I am always glad—even if I had to force myself to do it. Happiness can be sustained beyond the activity producing it.

Happiness is more than pleasure. Don't settle for an empty life of pleasure. Choose more. Rebel against the culture of pleasure and start actively seeking the happiness God created you for.

So, what will really make you happy?

Happiness is the result of right living. Honesty leads to happiness; dishonesty leads to misery. Caring for others leads to happiness; selfishness leads to unhappiness. Patience leads to happiness; impatience will make you miserable.

There are right and wrong ways to live your life. The culture tells us that there is no right and wrong. The culture says that what's wrong for you might be right for me. This is nonsense. Hitler's way was wrong. Mother Teresa's way was right.

But how do you know what is the right thing to do?

At a basic level, you just know. One of God's great gifts to you is conscience. Your conscience guides you in the way of right living so that you can celebrate the best version of yourself, and live your best life.

Very often we say we don't know what we should do, but we are lying to ourselves (and to others), because our conscience is telling us the right course of action but we are trying to ignore it.

Our regrets are born when we ignore our conscience.

But there may be a handful of times in your life when you legitimately don't know what the right thing to do is. It is for these times more than any other that God has given you another of his great gifts: reason.

I had dinner last week with some friends, Mike and Samantha. They have been married for two years and have been trying to have a baby,

but have not become pregnant. Their friends have been telling them about different types of fertility treatments, but they don't know if these treatments are part of God's dream for them. Mike and Jessica want to do the right thing, but they are not sure what the right thing to do is. This is a highly specialized and complex area of science and morality. To get to the truth they are going to need to study this issue.

This is a perfect example of why God gave you a beautiful mind. You have the ability to study an issue, search for the truth, think things through, seek out God's way, and act on the truth you discover.

If you want to make great decisions, just do the next right thing. Don't worry about what you have to do next week or next year; just do the next right thing right now.

Five, ten, fifty, one hundred times a day. Do the next right thing often enough and you will live a life uncommon, a life that is rich with inner peace and happiness.

WHO WAS Hitler?

Adolf Hitler (1889-1945) was the leader of the Nazi Party and Chancellor of Germany from 1933 to 1945. Hitler's was the diabolical mind behind the Holocaust; his regime was responsible for the deaths of six million Jews, as well as millions of others he and his followers considered racially or genetically inferior.

"THE TRUTH WILL SET YOU free"
JOHN 8:32

JOHN 8:32
KNOW IT: God created you for freedom and wants you to be free. Jesus is telling us that truth is essential for freedom and happiness.

THINK ABOUT IT: What lies are enslaving you?

LIVE IT: Make a conscious effort to align your actions with the truth this week.

32 **DECISION POINT** .... **WHAT'S HOLDING YOU BACK?** 33

STEP 4 JOURNAL

10 MIN

INSTRUCTIONS: Invite your class to open up to page 52 and take a few minutes in silence to journal their answers to those questions.

TIP

If some members of your class seem to be finished but others are still working, invite them to do the crossword puzzle at the end of the session.

STEP 5 ANNOUNCEMENTS

5 MIN

Tip

Thank them for coming. Never stop thanking them for coming. Tell them you are proud of the progress they are making. Remind them that you are praying for them every day. Encourage them to watch the videos again online or on the app, and to journal or do the crossword puzzle.

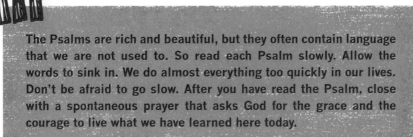

The Psalms are rich and beautiful, but they often contain language that we are not used to. So read each Psalm slowly. Allow the words to sink in. We do almost everything too quickly in our lives. Don't be afraid to go slow. After you have read the Psalm, close with a spontaneous prayer that asks God for the grace and the courage to live what we have learned here today.

5 MIN

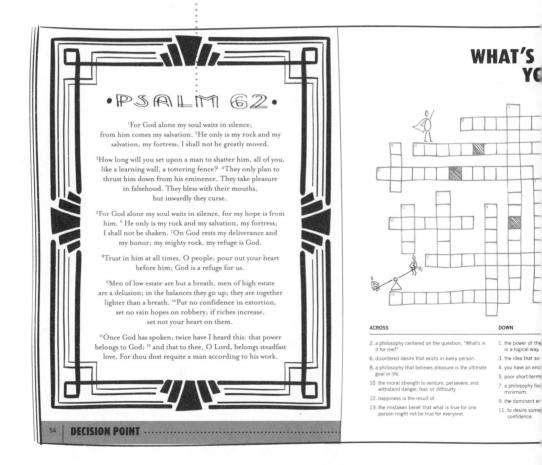

•PSALM 62•

¹For God alone my soul waits in silence;
from him comes my salvation. ²He only is my rock and my
salvation, my fortress; I shall not be greatly moved.

³How long will you set upon a man to shatter him, all of you,
like a learning wall, a tottering fence? ⁴They only plan to
thrust him down from his eminence. They take pleasure
in falsehood. They bless with their mouths,
but inwardly they curse.

⁵For God alone my soul waits in silence, for my hope is from
him. ⁶ He only is my rock and my salvation, my fortress;
I shall not be shaken. ⁷On God rests my deliverance and
my honor; my mighty rock, my refuge is God.

⁸Trust in him at all times, O people; pour out your heart
before him; God is a refuge for us.

⁹Men of low estate are but a breath, men of high estate
are a delusion; in the balances they go up; they are together
lighter than a breath. ¹⁰Put no confidence in extortion,
set no vain hopes on robbery; if riches increase,
set not your heart on them.

¹¹Once God has spoken; twice have I heard this: that power
belongs to God; ¹² and that to thee, O Lord, belongs steadfast
love. For thou dost requite a man according to his work.

54 | **DECISION POINT**

**WHAT'S
YO**

ACROSS

2. a philosophy centered on the question, "What's in it for me?"

6. disordered desire that exists in every person.

8. a philosophy that believes pleasure is the ultimate goal in life.

10. the moral strength to venture, persevere, and withstand danger, fear, or difficulty

12. happiness is the result of

13. the mistaken belief that what is true for one person might not be true for everyone.

DOWN

1. the power of the in a logical way.

3. the idea that so

4. you have an end

5. poor short-term

7. a philosophy fo minimum.

9. the dominant er

11. to desire some confidence.

The JESUS Question

Lord, catch me off guard today. Surprise me with some moment of beauty or pain. So that at least for the moment I may be startled into seeing that you are here in all your splendor, always and everywhere, barely hidden, beneath, beyond, within this life I breathe. Amen.

Frederick Buechner

QUICK SESSION OVERVIEW

STEP 1 WELCOME

STEP 2 OPENING PRAYER

STEP 3 ENGAGE – WATCH & DISCUSS

STEP 4 JOURNAL

STEP 5 ANNOUNCEMENTS

STEP 6 CLOSING PRAYER

SESSION THREE: THE JESUS QUESTION

Objectives:

- To encourage candidates to rediscover Jesus and to reassess the role he should be playing in their lives.

- To teach candidates that Jesus and his teachings are the answer to the problems we face in our lives and in the world.

- To help candidates recognize the power and importance of having a personal relationship with Jesus.

Start on time. If people are late, they are late. Systems drive behavior—if you want them to be on time, you need to start on time.

Remind them of one of the key points from the previous session, just like TV shows start with, "Previously on . . ." followed by a short highlights reel from the most recent episode.

Ask them what they remember from the previous session.

Engage them constantly. They may resist, but in truth they yearn for this.

LEADER GUIDE KEY

TIME-ICON: This icon serves as a guide to help you plan approximately how long each activity will take.

[WB5] This code serves as a reference to point you to the page in the Workbook where you can find the related activity/content.

Example: **[WB5]** *points you to page 5 in the Workbook*

The flag icon is the halfway mark and suggests a good breaking point if your program runs twenty-four classes (or approximately 60 minutes) instead of twelve 120 minute classes.

Tip

Each of the prayers has been selected to do exactly what this prayer asks the Lord to do: catch us off guard. These prayers are real and approachable. The language they use is practical.

Begin with the Sign of the Cross, invite them to close their eyes, and read the opening prayer slowly and deliberately. Then give them thirty seconds in silence to reflect on the prayer and what God is saying to them through it.

3 MIN

Lord, catch me off guard today. Surprise me with some moment of beauty or pain. So that at least for the moment I may be startled into seeing that you are here in all your splendor, always and everywhere, barely hidden, beneath, beyond, within this life I breathe. Amen.

Frederick Buechner

SESSION 3 INTRODUCTION

WATCH VIDEO

4 MIN

TIP: Ask them if they ever think about Judas and how he got to be the way he was. Tell them that this short film gave you a perspective on Judas and on yourself that you had never really considered before.

DISCUSSION QUESTION

6 MIN

1) What is the one idea in this short film that you found most helpful?

STEP 3 ENGAGE: WATCH & DISCUSS

CONTINUED...

SESSION 3.1 WHO IS JESUS?

WATCH VIDEO

9 MIN

3.1 WHO IS JESUS?

DISCUSSION QUESTIONS [WB62]

10 MIN

Tip These are big questions. They are life-changing questions. Tell them that. "We are just taking a few minutes to start exploring these questions together now. But these are big questions that you will spend the rest of your life revisiting."

1) How did this session change the way you see Jesus?

2) How did Jesus change the world?

3) The Jesus question is, "Who do you say that I am?" (Mark 8:29) If Jesus came to your house to visit today and asked you this question, what would your answer be?

EXERCISE

Invite a student to read **"Who Is the Messiah?"** [WB60]
Invite another student to read **"The Jesus Prophecies."** [WB69]
When both have been read, ask the students to speak
about their reactions to each piece.

5 MIN

TIP! Talk about how your relationship with Jesus has evolved over the course of your life. Talk about the difference between who you are today and who you were before you really knew Jesus.

I BELIEVE IN THE HOLY SPIRIT, THE LORD, THE GIVER OF LIFE, WHO PROCEEDS FROM THE FATHER AND THE SON, WHO WITH THE FATHER AND THE SON IS ADORED AND GLORIFIED, WHO HAS SPOKEN THROUGH TH

WHO IS THE Messiah -?-

THROUGHOUT THE OLD TESTAMENT, REFERENCES ARE MADE TO THE MESSIAH, THE HOLY ONE OF GOD, WHO WOULD COME AND SAVE GOD'S PEOPLE. AS CHRISTIANS **WE BELIEVE THAT JESUS IS THE MESSIAH.**

Notice Jesus didn't ask the disciples who they thought he was the first day he met them. By the time he asked, they had been at his side for almost three years.

So perhaps before you answer the Jesus question, we should take another look at Jesus, who he is, why he came, what he really taught, and what all of that means to you in the modern world.

The culture wants to reduce Jesus to just a *nice guy.* This is tragic. So, who is Jesus?

There are many ways to answer the question. He is a Galilean. A Jew. A carpenter. An itinerant preacher. A miracle worker. The Son of God. The King of Kings. The Christ. The Savior of the world. The chosen one. The Messiah.

C. S. Lewis, one of the great Christian writers of the twentieth century and the creator of the Narnia series, says we only really have three choices when it comes to Jesus: He is a either a liar, a lunatic, or the Messiah he claims to be.

Other major world religions acknowledge Jesus as a great teacher or a great prophet—which seems very accommodating and tolerant—but there are several problems with this position.

First, Jesus never claimed to be a great teacher or a great prophet. He claimed to be the long awaited Messiah. If he isn't the Messiah, he is either a liar or a lunatic—but not a great teacher and prophet. *These things are incongruent.*

Let's get clear. If Jesus is not the Messiah, *he is the biggest liar who ever lived.* You cannot be the biggest liar in history and still be a great teacher and prophet. These things are incongruent.

And more than being a liar, if Jesus is not the Christ, he perpetrated *the biggest fraud in human history.*

There is the option that he was a lunatic, that he was mentally ill. Asylums are full of people with the "Messiah complex," but there is no historic record of anyone of any credibility claiming to be the Messiah before Jesus, and I suspect you cannot name someone who has claimed to be the Savior of the world since. The Messiah complex is a post Jesus phenomenon.

If Jesus was a lunatic, could the early Christians have kept that a secret? The scale of the conspiracy that would be required to conceal Jesus as a lunatic makes it more than improbable. And if he was just a lunatic, they could have easily proved that and simply locked him up. There would have been no need to crucify him, as he would have been easily discredited. If they could have proved he was a lunatic, they would have had no reason to feel threatened by him, and no reason to kill him. But he was considered by both the secular and the religious authorities of his time to be much more dangerous than a simple lunatic.

Who is Jesus? He is the Galilean carpenter who became an itinerant preacher, who turned water into wine, made the lame walk and the blind see, walked on water, multiplied a handful of loaves and fishes to feed thousands, got under the skin of secular and religious leaders of the day, was executed on a cross, was buried in a borrowed tomb, and three days later rose from the dead. Jesus wasn't a great teacher; he was the greatest teacher. He wasn't a great prophet; he was the greatest prophet. But more importantly, Jesus is the Christ, the long-awaited Messiah.

Now let's take a look at what all this means to you.

WHAT IS A PROPHET?

A PERSON WHO ANNOUNCES THE WILL OF GOD.

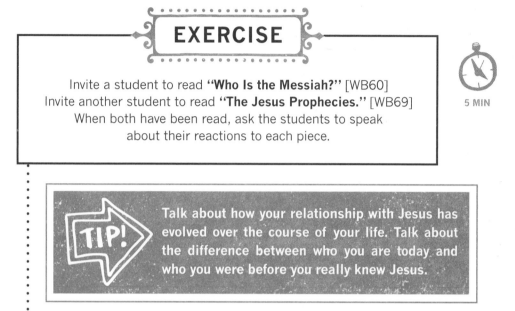

miracle worker

THE CHRIST THE MESSIAH CARPENTER

KING OF KINGS Galilean Jew

SON OF GOD THE CHOOSEN ONE

ITINERANT PREACHER

SAVIOR of the WORLD

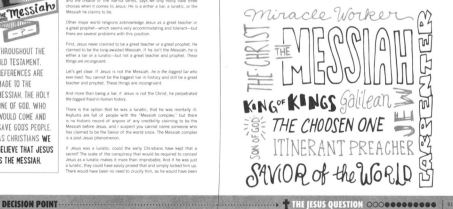

SESSION 3.2 THE PROBLEM AND THE SOLUTION

WATCH VIDEO

7 MIN

3.2 the PROBLEM and the SOLUTION

> **TIP** Introduce the video. "Have you ever wondered why the world is a bit of a mess? This next video does a great job of explaining that."

10 MIN

DISCUSSION QUESTIONS [WB67]

1) In many ways the world is an incredible place, but in lots of other ways it is a mess. In what ways is the world a mess?

2) How did the world get to be such a mess?

3) What is sin? How does it affect you?

SESSION 3.3 JESUS WAS A RADICAL

WATCH VIDEO

8 MIN

TIP

If they seem restless, distracted, or lifeless, take a few moments before this next video to get them moving. It may seem counterintuitive to think that moving would help them sit still and focus, but it works. Ask everyone to change chairs and sit as far away as possible from the chair they are in at the moment.

DISCUSSION QUESTIONS [WB73]

10 MIN

1) Who do you know who take the teachings of Jesus seriously, allowing those lessons to direct the way they live their lives?

2) How do the teachings of Jesus challenge you to radically change your life?

3) What is agape love? How is it different from the way movies, music, and the media portray love?

EXERCISE: ONE SOLITARY LIFE

Read "One Solitary Life." Then ask the students to identify one thing about Jesus that the poem points out that they had never thought about before. [WB82]

5 MIN

 **Tip**

This is a powerful piece. Don't rob it of its power. Read it a couple of times before class. Take a moment to get the class quiet before you begin. Invite them to close their eyes if they seem distracted. Read it slowly, deliberately. Let the words sink in.

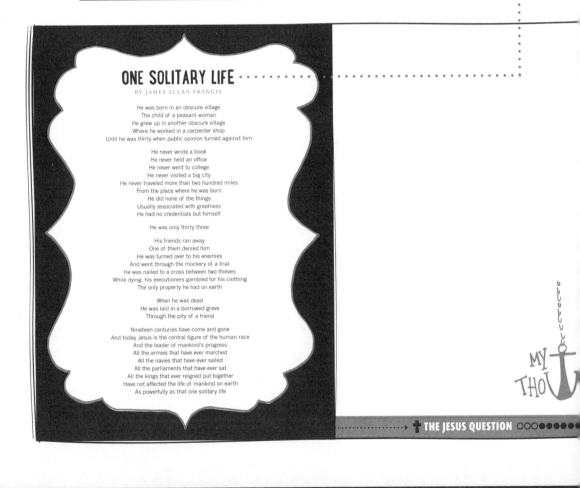

ONE SOLITARY LIFE

BY JAMES ALLAN FRANCIS

He was born in an obscure village
The child of a peasant woman
He grew up in another obscure village
Where he worked in a carpenter shop
Until he was thirty when public opinion turned against him

He never wrote a book
He never held an office
He never went to college
He never visited a big city
He never traveled more than two hundred miles
From the place where he was born
He did none of the things
Usually associated with greatness
He had no credentials but himself

He was only thirty three

His friends ran away
One of them denied him
He was turned over to his enemies
And went through the mockery of a trial
He was nailed to a cross between two thieves
While dying, his executioners gambled for his clothing
The only property he had on earth

When he was dead
He was laid in a borrowed grave
Through the pity of a friend

Nineteen centuries have come and gone
And today Jesus is the central figure of the human race
And the leader of mankind's progress
All the armies that have ever marched
All the navies that have ever sailed
All the parliaments that have ever sat
All the kings that ever reigned put together
Have not affected the life of mankind on earth
As powerfully as that one solitary life

MY
THOU

✝ **THE JESUS QUESTION** ○○○●●●●●●

SESSION 3.4 SECOND CHANCES

WATCH VIDEO

Introduce the video by saying that we all need a second chance from time to time.

4 MIN

DISCUSSION QUESTIONS [WB78]

10 MIN

1) Grace is the help God gives us to respond to his call and to do what is good and right. In what part of your life do you need God's grace most today?

2) How do you imagine you would be different if you went to reconciliation once a month?

3) We all need to be forgiven by God and others, and we all have people we need to forgive. In the Our Father we pray, "Forgive us our trespasses as we forgive those who trespass against us." Whom is God calling you to forgive today?

EXERCISE VIRTUE IN FOCUS

5 MIN

TIP

Every session highlights a virtue. Invite a candidate to read the **Virtue in Focus** section. Choose one of the questions from the section and ask the candidates to share their answers. [WB77]

SUBSTANTIAL WITH THE FATHER; THROUGH HIM ALL THINGS WERE MADE, FOR US MEN AND FOR OUR SALVATION HE CAME DOWN FROM HEAVEN, AND BY THE HOLY SPIRIT WAS INCAR-

3.4 SECOND ★ CHANCES

We spoke earlier about God's dream for you to become the-best-version-of-yourself. We also spoke about how sometimes we want to do the right thing, but we find ourselves doing the complete opposite.

You may be too young right now, but there will come a time in your life when you will try to overcome a bad habit but cannot. You will try and try again, but over and over you will fail. And then you will discover that some things cannot be done merely by willpower and your own strength and abilities. On this day you will discover your need for **grace**.

What is grace? Grace is the help God gives us to respond to his call, and to do what is good and right.

Grace gets us beyond the Paul dilemma: "I do not do the good I want, but the evil I do not want is what I do."

Ask an alcoholic who has tried to stop drinking and he will tell you that he tried and tried on his own, and failed. Finally, he surrendered to God, and *grace* allowed him to quit drinking and stay sober.

We all come up against bad habits we cannot shake at different times. These are the great intersections of our lives, the moments when we choose to surrender to God's grace or hold on stubbornly to our old self-destructive ways.

The truth is, you cannot become the-best-version-of-yourself on your own. You need grace. The fullness of the invitation is to become the-best-version-of-yourself in Jesus.

Without grace nothing is possible.

With all the talk of sin in the previous section, you may not be feeling so good about yourself. That's good. Seriously, that's really good. It means that you are in touch with your conscience. This is a sign of spiritual life.

Fortunately as Christians we believe in the forgiveness of sin. This is where grace and sin intersect.

We all need a fresh start from time to time.

One of the greatest sources of grace is the sacrament of **Reconciliation**. I am not going to give you a long lecture about it. I am just going to encourage you to go to Reconciliation . . . and to go regularly.

I try to go once a month. I need the grace. I need to take an honest look at myself. I need to be held accountable; it brings the best out of me. I need the spiritual coaching and guidance that I get in the sacrament of Reconciliation.

It's good for me and I love the peace that fills my heart when the priest says the words of absolution:

"God, the Father of mercies, through the death and resurrection of his Son has reconciled the world to himself and sent the Holy Spirit among us for the forgiveness of sins; through the ministry of the Church may God give you pardon and peace, and I absolve you from your sins in the name of the Father, and of the Son, and of the Holy Spirit. Amen."

The peace that comes from having our sins forgiven is a peace the world cannot give. Do you have that peace? If you don't, maybe it's time you made a good confession.

VIRTUE IN FOCUS

Joy [joi]
A state of happiness that is independent of situations or circumstances

What brings you joy?

Who is the most joyful person you know?

What can you do to increase your capacity for joy and to bring more joy to others?

SESSION 3.5 DECISION POINT

WATCH VIDEO

3.5 DECISION point

Tip

Encourage them. Some of your candidates may have no genuine encouragement in their lives.

3 MIN

EXERCISE: Know It. Think About It. Live It.

TIP

Encourage them to bring a Bible to class. Throughout the program we will highlight verses from the Bible in exactly the same way: **KNOW IT. THINK ABOUT IT. LIVE IT.** We will only explore one of these versions together, but each time you do, encourage them to open their Bibles and find the passage. Getting young people comfortable with a Bible in their hands is another huge leap in their spiritual journey. [WB72]

5 MIN

BORN OF THE FATHER BEFORE ALL AGES, GOD FROM GOD, LIGHT FROM LIGHT, TRUE GOD FROM TRUE GOD.

"I am the Way, the Truth, and the Life." John 14: 5-7

KNOW IT: What three things did Jesus say he is?

THINK ABOUT IT: Would you be a better version of yourself if you followed Jesus WAY, accepted his TRUTH, and embraced his LIFE?

LIVE IT: Allow Jesus to direct what you do sometime today!

But Jesus doesn't just love that way; he calls us to love in the same way. (I told you he was radical.)

On Sunday at Mass, after the Gospel has been read, I ask myself, "If I lived this one Gospel reading 100 percent, how much would my life change?" The answer is the same every week: radically.

There is a gap between my life and the life God invites me to live. There is a gap between the person I am and the person God created me to be. I have a long way to go. But I have started and I hope you will join me in the journey.

Most people think they are pretty good Christians. I even know non-Christians who think they are pretty good Christians. But compared to what? Compared to Jesus? No, most people don't use that as their measuring stick. Compared to the Gospel? Most people don't use that as their measuring stick either. Most compare themselves to what they see on television or to their peers. In most cases today this can be setting the bar very low indeed.

If you really want to explore the question of the best way to live, I recommend you get yourself a Bible and just start by reading the Gospel of Matthew. Read it slowly. Think about what you're reading. This way you will save yourself a lot of heartache and discover the path that leads to lasting happiness in this life and eternal happiness with God in the next life.

Along the way you will also discover the real Jesus, and you might discover he is very, very different to what you had previously thought.

ask yourself...

IF I LIVED THIS ONE Gospel READING 100%, HOW MUCH WOULD MY LIFE CHANGE?

RADICALLY.

Discussion Questions

1. WHO DO YOU KNOW WHO TAKE THE TEACHINGS OF JESUS SERIOUSLY, ALLOWING THOSE LESSONS TO DIRECT THE WAY THEY LIVE THEIR LIVES?

2. HOW DO THE TEACHINGS OF JESUS CHALLENGE YOU TO RADICALLY CHANGE YOUR LIFE?

3. WHAT IS AGAPE LOVE? HOW IS IT DIFFERENT FROM THE WAY MOVIES, MUSIC, AND THE MEDIA PORTRAY LOVE?

 **STEP 4** **JOURNAL**

8 MIN

INSTRUCTIONS: Invite your class to open up to page 81 and take a few minutes in silence to journal their answers to those questions.

TIP

There is something powerful about writing down our deepest thoughts. Encourage them to make time to journal, not just now but for the rest of their lives.

 **STEP 5** **ANNOUNCEMENTS**

3 MIN

Tip

Thank them for coming. Remind them you will be praying for them during the week. Remember, if you cannot convince them that you care about them, you will not be able to deliver a life-changing experience.

Encourage them to watch the videos again online or on the app. Give them examples of when they could do this during their day. "Watch one each night before you go to bed." "Watch one each time you have a gap in your day."

This time let's mix it up. Start with a spontaneous prayer and then lead into the Psalm. Prayer is powerful. Prayer can change a person's life. Pray with power. Allow the power of God—Father, Son, and Holy Spirit—to flow through you. Ask God to fill you with the Holy Spirit so that you can impact and influence the young people before you in powerful ways.

5 MIN

Psalm 23

[1] The Lord is my shepherd, I shall not want;

[2] he makes me lie down in green pastures.
He leads me beside still waters;

[3] he restores my soul. He leads me in paths
of righteousness for his name's sake.

[4] Even though I walk through the valley
of the shadow of death, I fear no evil;
for thou art with me; thy rod and thy staff,
they comfort me.

[5] Thou preparest a table before me
in the presence of my enemies; thou anointest
my head with oil, my cup overflows.

[6] Surely goodness and mercy shall follow me
all the days of my life; and I shall dwell in
the house of the Lord for ever.

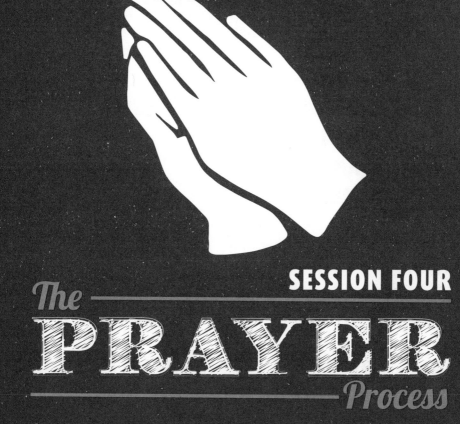

The PRAYER Process

God, grant me the serenity to accept the things I cannot change, courage to change the things I can, and wisdom to know the difference. Living one day at a time, enjoying one moment at a time, accepting hardships as the pathway to peace, taking, as Jesus did, this sinful world as it is, not as I would have it, trusting that you will make all things right, if I surrender to your will, so that I may be reasonably happy in this life, and supremely happy with you forever in the next. Amen.

The Serenity Prayer

QUICK SESSION OVERVIEW

STEP 1 | **WELCOME**
STEP 2 | **OPENING PRAYER**
STEP 3 | **ENGAGE – WATCH & DISCUSS**
STEP 4 | **JOURNAL**
STEP 5 | **ANNOUNCEMENTS**
STEP 6 | **CLOSING PRAYER**

SESSION FOUR: THE PRAYER PROCESS

Objectives:

- To teach the candidates how to pray.

- To demonstrate that the way prayer helps is by helping us discover God's will for our lives, and that we cannot ever truly be happy outside of God's will.

- To encourage candidates to develop a daily routine of prayer.

Whether it has been a week or a month since you last met with them, ask the candidates to tell you the best thing that's happened since you were last together. Take an interest in their lives. We listen most to the people we believe have our best interests at heart. The more you convince them that you are interested in them as individuals, the more they will listen to what you have to say.

✳ LEADER GUIDE KEY

TIME-ICON: This icon serves as a guide to help you plan approximately how long each activity will take.

[WB5] This code serves as a reference to point you to the page in the Workbook where you can find the related activity/content.

Example: **[WB5]** *points you to page 5 in the Workbook*

The flag icon is the halfway mark and suggests a good breaking point if your program runs twenty-four classes (or approximately 60 minutes) instead of twelve 120 minute classes.

Tip

Take a moment to get them quiet.

Now, speak to them about why quiet time is important in your life. The more specific you can be, the more they will latch on to this habit. How does quiet time make you a better person, friend, husband, wife, father, mother?

Begin with the Sign of the Cross, invite them to close their eyes, and read the opening prayer slowly and deliberately. Then give them thirty seconds in silence to reflect on the prayer and what God is saying to them through it.

3 MIN

God, grant me the serenity to accept the things I cannot change, courage to change the things I can, and wisdom to know the difference. Living one day at a time, enjoying one moment at a time, accepting hardships as the pathway to peace, taking, as Jesus did, this sinful world as it is, not as I would have it, trusting that you will make all things right, if I surrender to your will, so that I may be reasonably happy in this life, and supremely happy with you forever in the next. Amen.

· ———— *The Serenity Prayer* ———— ·

STEP 3 ENGAGE: WATCH & DISCUSS

SESSION 4 INTRODUCTION

WATCH VIDEO

4 MIN

TIP:

We spend hundreds of thousands of hours watching television during our lives. But how often do you get up from watching TV and think, "That program helped me become a-better-version-of-myself!" Probably not that often. Point out how rare it is that the programs we watch actually help us grow and improve.

DISCUSSION QUESTION

6 MIN

1) What is the one idea in this short film that you found most helpful?

SESSION 4.1 WHY PRAY?

WATCH VIDEO

4 MIN

DISCUSSION QUESTIONS [WB88]

10 MIN

Tip Involve everyone. Ask males and females an equal number of questions. Look around the room. Move the conversation around the classroom, trying to involve as much of the class as possible.

1) Whom do you talk to every day? Why?

2) Do you pray? How often? How do you feel after you pray?

3) Do you think you would be happier if you made time to pray each day?

EXERCISE

Exercise: Invite a student to read **"Who Was Saint Teresa of Avila?"** Ask the students what they think it would be like to live a life of prayer and silence as a cloistered nun. [WB95]

5 MIN

TIP!

When someone is speaking, give him or her your full attention. Make sure they know by your body language that you are deeply interested in what they are saying—and by extension, deeply interested in them.

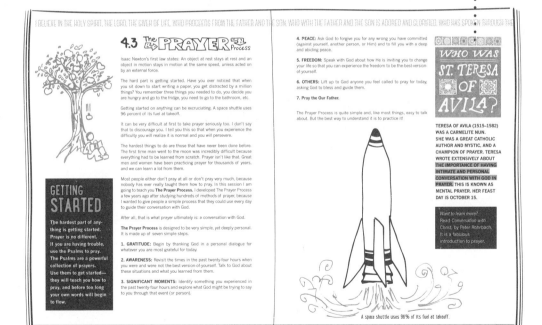

I BELIEVE IN THE HOLY SPIRIT, THE LORD, THE GIVER OF LIFE, WHO PROCEEDS FROM THE FATHER AND THE SON, WHO WITH THE FATHER AND THE SON IS ADORED AND GLORIFIED, WHO HAS SPOKEN THROUGH THE

4.3 The PRAYER Process

Isaac Newton's first law states: An object at rest stays at rest and an object in motion stays in motion at the same speed, unless acted on by an external force.

The hard part is getting started. Have you ever noticed that when you sit down to start writing a paper, you get distracted by a million things? You remember three things you needed to do, you decide you are hungry and go to the fridge, you need to go to the bathroom, etc.

Getting started on anything can be excruciating. A space shuttle uses 96 percent of its fuel at takeoff.

It can be very difficult at first to take prayer seriously too. I don't say that to discourage you. I tell you this so that when you experience the difficulty you will realize it is normal and you will persevere.

The hardest things to do are those that have never been done before. The first time man went to the moon was incredibly difficult because everything had to be learned from scratch. Prayer isn't like that. Great men and women have been practicing prayer for thousands of years, and we can learn a lot from them.

Most people either don't pray at all or don't pray very much, because nobody has ever really taught them how to pray. In this session I am going to teach you **The Prayer Process**. I developed The Prayer Process a few years ago after studying hundreds of methods of prayer, because I wanted to give people a simple process that they could use every day to guide their conversation with God.

After all, that is what prayer ultimately is: a conversation with God.

The Prayer Process is designed to be very simple, yet deeply personal. It is made up of seven simple steps.

1. GRATITUDE: Begin by thanking God in a personal dialogue for whatever you are most grateful for today.

2. AWARENESS: Revisit the times in the past twenty-four hours when you were and were not the-best-version-of-yourself. Talk to God about these situations and what you learned from them.

3. SIGNIFICANT MOMENTS: Identify something you experienced in the past twenty-four hours and explore what God might be trying to say to you through that event (or person).

GETTING STARTED

The hardest part of anything is getting started. Prayer is no different. If you are having trouble, use the Psalms to pray. The Psalms are a powerful collection of prayers. Use them to get started—they will teach you how to pray, and before too long your own words will begin to flow.

4. PEACE: Ask God to forgive you for any wrong you have committed (against yourself, another person, or Him) and to fill you with a deep and abiding peace.

5. FREEDOM: Speak with God about how He is inviting you to change your life so that you can experience the freedom to be the-best-version-of-yourself.

6. OTHERS: Lift up to God anyone you feel called to pray for today, asking God to bless and guide them.

7. Pray the Our Father.

The Prayer Process is quite simple and, like most things, easy to talk about. But the best way to understand it is to practice it!

WHO WAS ST. TERESA OF AVILA?

TERESA OF AVILA (1515–1582) WAS A CARMELITE NUN. SHE WAS A GREAT CATHOLIC AUTHOR AND MYSTIC, AND A CHAMPION OF PRAYER. TERESA WROTE EXTENSIVELY ABOUT **THE IMPORTANCE OF HAVING INTIMATE AND PERSONAL CONVERSATION WITH GOD IN PRAYER.** THIS IS KNOWN AS MENTAL PRAYER. HER FEAST DAY IS OCTOBER 15.

Want to learn more? Read Conversation with Christ, by Peter Rohrbach. It is a fabulous introduction to prayer.

A space shuttle uses 96% of its fuel at takeoff.

SESSION 4.2 **THE BIG QUESTION**

6 MIN

WATCH VIDEO

4.2 THE **BIG** QUESTION

T I P

Introduce the video by saying something like, "This next short film is called 'The Big Question.' What do you think the big question is?"

---

10 MIN

DISCUSSION QUESTIONS [WB92]

1) Describe a time when someone challenged you to do something that would help you become the-best-version-of-yourself. How did you respond?

2) Have you ever asked God the big question: "What do you think I should do?" If you have, what happened? If you have never asked God the big question, why not?

3) If you spent ten minutes a day in prayer every day for the next month, how do you think you might be different a month from now?

WATCH VIDEO

5 MIN

10 MIN

TIP

Introduce the video by asking them: Has anyone ever really taught you how to pray? Tell them about how you learned to pray and how you wish you could have had access to a video like the one they are about to experience when you were their age.

DISCUSSION QUESTIONS [WB96]

1) Has anyone ever taught you how to pray? Who? When?

2) Which of the seven steps in the prayer process intrigued you the most? Why?

3) If you were going to set aside ten minutes to pray at the same time every day, what time of day would be best for you?

EXERCISE: THE GEOGRAPHY OF PRAYER · · · · · · · · · · · ·

6 MIN

Ask one of your class members to read aloud "The Geography of Prayer."
Go through the regions of the world that we pray for during each decade
of the Rosary. Ask the students to name countries in that region. Then ask
them how they think life is different in those places. [WB106]

Tip

Left to our own devices, most of us would become fairly self-centered.
We cannot grow spiritually unless we get outside ourselves, and put other
people and their legitimate needs ahead of our selfish and sometimes
reckless wants. This exercise is designed to give perspective about how
difficult life is for people in other parts of the world. The result of this
perspective should be gratitude and a desire to help others.

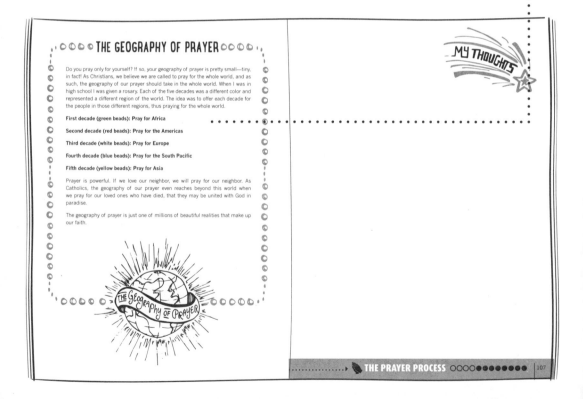

THE GEOGRAPHY OF PRAYER

Do you pray only for yourself? If so, your geography of prayer is pretty small—tiny,
in fact! As Christians, we believe we are called to pray for the whole world, and as
such, the geography of our prayer should take in the whole world. When I was in
high school I was given a rosary. Each of the five decades was a different color and
represented a different region of the world. The idea was to offer each decade for
the people in those different regions, thus praying for the whole world.

First decade (green beads): Pray for Africa

Second decade (red beads): Pray for the Americas

Third decade (white beads): Pray for Europe

Fourth decade (blue beads): Pray for the South Pacific

Fifth decade (yellow beads): Pray for Asia

Prayer is powerful. If we love our neighbor, we will pray for our neighbor. As
Catholics, the geography of our prayer even reaches beyond this world when
we pray for our loved ones who have died, that they may be united with God in
paradise.

The geography of prayer is just one of millions of beautiful realities that make up
our faith.

MY THOUGHTS

▶ THE PRAYER PROCESS ○○○○●●●●●●●● 107

SESSION 4.4 **THE BEST WAY TO LEARN**

WATCH VIDEO

 Tell them that this is an experiential short film designed to help them actually experience The Prayer Process.

10 MIN

DISCUSSION QUESTIONS [WB101]

10 MIN

1) What are you most grateful for today?

2) What surprised you the most as you practiced the prayer process?

3) Now that you have been taught how to pray, what is most likely to get in the way of developing prayer as a daily habit in your life?

EXERCISE VIRTUE IN FOCUS

5 MIN

TIP

This session highlights the virtue of perseverance. Invite a candidate to read the **Virtue in Focus** section. Discuss with the class why it is so difficult to persevere and what techniques they have learned to help push themselves when they are tempted to quit. [WB99]

THE PROPHETS. I BELIEVE IN ONE, HOLY, CATHOLIC AND APOSTOLIC CHURCH. I CONFESS ONE BAPTISM FOR THE FORGIVENESS OF SINS AND I LOOK FORWARD TO THE RESURRECTION

4.4 The Best Way to learn

You get good at riding a bicycle, not by reading a book about bikes or listening to a lecture about riding techniques, but by actually riding a bicycle. Sure, the book and the lecture can be helpful, but ultimately you will hone your skills by spending time on the bike.

The same is true for prayer. It's good to talk about it and to read books about it, but at some point the best thing to do is just try it and see what you learn from actually praying.

There are two reasons most people don't pray: nobody ever taught them and they don't know where to start. The Prayer Process solves both of these problems. It teaches us how to pray and it gives us a simple step-by-step process, so we know exactly where to start.

What I would like to do now is to walk you through the process while you actually practice it. I'll keep talking to you, guiding you through the process, but there won't be anything to watch here on the screen. So, let's start by closing our eyes.

Now, get comfortable, so that you can be still and quiet for a few minutes, and take some deep breaths. Breathe in deep, and breathe out any stress or anxiety that you have in your life today.

Now, let's begin...

In the name of the Father, and of the Son, and of the Holy Spirit. Amen.

The first step in The Prayer Process is... GRATITUDE: Begin by thanking God in a personal dialogue for whatever you are most grateful for today.

What are you grateful for at this time in your life? Talk to God about that. Don't just think about it. Have a mental conversation with God about everyone and everything you are grateful for today...

The second step in The Prayer Process is... AWARENESS: Revisit the times in the past twenty-four hours when you were and were not the-best-version-of-yourself. Talk to God about these situations and what you learned from them.

Recall a time in the past twenty-four hours when you were the-best-version-of-yourself, even if it was just for a moment... Talk to God about that situation... tell him if it was easy or difficult... and how you felt...

Now bring to mind a time in the past twenty-four hours when you were not the-best-version-of-yourself... Talk to God about why you

did what you did... tell him how you felt at the time... and how you felt after... and talk to him about how you are going to try to handle situations like that differently in the future...

The third step in the process is... SIGNIFICANT MOMENTS: Identify something you experienced in the past twenty-four hours and explore what God might be trying to say to you through that event (or person).

How have you experienced God in the past twenty-four hours? Did you sense that God was trying to tell you something through a person or something that happened? Talk to God about that now... again, try to go beyond just thinking about these things and have a mental conversation with God...

The fourth step in the process is... PEACE: Ask God to forgive you for any wrong you have committed (against yourself, another person, or Him) and to fill you with a deep and abiding peace.

Are you carrying around guilt or shame over something? God is your Father and he loves you deeply, ask him right now to forgive you and fill you with a deep, deep peace.

The fifth step in The Prayer Process is... FREEDOM: Speak with God about how He is inviting you to change your life so that you can experience the freedom to be-the-best-version-of-yourself.

God loves you as you are today, but he loves you too much to let you stay this way. How do you sense God is calling you to change and grow? Talk to him about that... now ask him to give you the courage and strength to make this change in your life...

The sixth step in the process is... OTHERS: Lift up to God anyone you feel called to pray for today, asking God to bless and guide them.

Who do you want God to bless in a special way today? Talk to God about each of these people... and vocalize the specific ways you would like God to bless them... Take your time... Slowly pray for the people in your life... one at a time...

The final step of The Prayer Process is to pray the Our Father. It is a prayer most of us have been praying all our lives, but if we really comprehended the words of this prayer we would not be able to finish it without weeping for joy. So, let's pray it together, out loud, slowly and deliberately...

Our Father...

GET THE APP!

VIRTUE IN FOCUS

Per·se·ver·ance
[pur-suh-veer-uh ns]

Continued effort to do or achieve something despite difficulties, delays, failure, or opposition.

Developing a dynamic prayer life requires perseverance more than anything else. **Just keep showing up.** Some days you will feel like praying and many days you will not, but if you keep showing up you will develop a phenomenal friendship with God.

INT

▶ THE PRAYER PROCESS ○○○○●●●●●●●● 99

SESSION 4.5 DECISION POINT

WATCH VIDEO

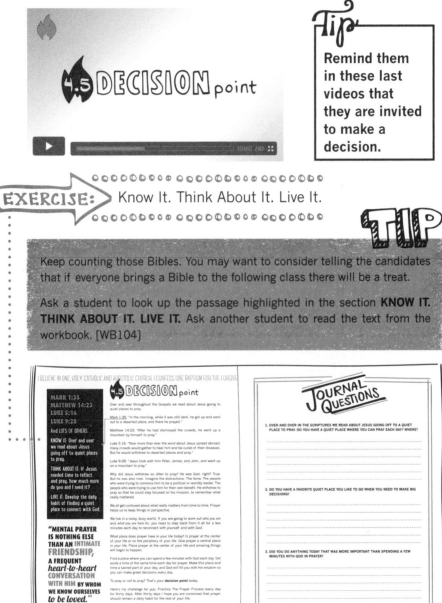

4.5 DECISION point

Tip

Remind them in these last videos that they are invited to make a decision.

3 MIN

EXERCISE: Know It. Think About It. Live It.

TIP

Keep counting those Bibles. You may want to consider telling the candidates that if everyone brings a Bible to the following class there will be a treat.

Ask a student to look up the passage highlighted in the section **KNOW IT. THINK ABOUT IT. LIVE IT.** Ask another student to read the text from the workbook. [WB104]

5 MIN

I BELIEVE IN ONE, HOLY, CATHOLIC AND APOSTOLIC CHURCH. I CONFESS ONE BAPTISM FOR THE FORGIVE

4.5 DECISION point

MARK 1:35
MATTHEW 14:23
LUKE 5:16
LUKE 9:28
And LOTS of OTHERS

KNOW IT: Over and over we read about Jesus going off to quiet places to pray.

THINK ABOUT IT: If Jesus needed time to reflect and pray, how much more do you and I need it?

LIVE IT: Develop the daily habit of finding a quiet place to connect with God.

"MENTAL PRAYER IS NOTHING ELSE THAN AN INTIMATE FRIENDSHIP, A FREQUENT heart-to-heart CONVERSATION WITH HIM BY WHOM WE KNOW OURSELVES to be loved."

—Saint Teresa of Avila

Over and over throughout the Gospels we read about Jesus going to quiet places to pray.

Mark 1:35: "In the morning, while it was still dark, he got up and went out to a deserted place, and there he prayed."

Matthew 14:23: "After he had dismissed the crowds, he went up a mountain by himself to pray."

Luke 5:16: "Now more than ever the word about Jesus spread abroad; many crowds would gather to hear him and be cured of their diseases. But he would withdraw to deserted places and pray."

Luke 9:28: "Jesus took with him Peter, James, and John, and went up on a mountain to pray."

Why did Jesus withdraw so often to pray? He was God, right? True. But he was also man. Imagine the distractions. The fame. The people who were trying to convince him to be a political or worldly leader. The people who were trying to use him for their own benefit. He withdrew to pray so that he could stay focused on his mission, to remember what really mattered.

We all get confused about what really matters from time to time. Prayer helps us to keep things in perspective.

We live in a noisy, busy world. If you are going to work out who you are and what you are here for, you need to step back from it all for a few minutes each day to reconnect with yourself and with God.

What place does prayer have in your life today? Is prayer at the center of your life or on the periphery of your life. Give prayer a central place in your life. Place prayer at the center of your life and amazing things will begin to happen.

Find a place where you can spend a few minutes with God each day. Set aside a time at the same time each day for prayer. Make this place and time a sacred part of your day, and God will fill you with his wisdom so you can make great decisions every day.

To pray or not to pray? That's your **decision point** today.

Here's my challenge for you: Practice The Prayer Process every day for thirty days. After thirty days I hope you are convinced that prayer should remain a daily habit for the rest of your life.

JOURNAL Questions

1. OVER AND OVER IN THE SCRIPTURES WE READ ABOUT JESUS GOING OFF TO A QUIET PLACE TO PRAY. DO YOU HAVE A QUIET PLACE WHERE YOU CAN PRAY EACH DAY? WHERE?

2. DO YOU HAVE A FAVORITE QUIET PLACE YOU LIKE TO GO WHEN YOU NEED TO MAKE BIG DECISIONS?

3. DID YOU DO ANYTHING TODAY THAT WAS MORE IMPORTANT THAN SPENDING A FEW MINUTES WITH GOD IN PRAYER?

104 **DECISION POINT**

THE PRAYER PROCESS 105

 **STEP 4** # JOURNAL

10 MIN

INSTRUCTIONS: Invite your class to open up to page 105 and take a few minutes in silence to journal their answers to those questions.

TIP

Routine is beautiful. We spend a lot of our lives rebelling against it, but the truth is routines bring out the best in us. Encourage the candidates to develop healthy routines in their lives, and to make journaling one of them.

STEP 5 # ANNOUNCEMENTS

3 MIN

~~~~~ *Tip* ~~~~~

Smile. Thank them for coming. Remind them you will be praying for them during the week. Some of the candidates might not have anyone in their lives who really cares deeply about them. You don't know what is happening in their hearts and in their lives. So reassure them that they are not alone.

Once is not enough. We learn by repetition. Encourage them to watch the videos again online or on the app.

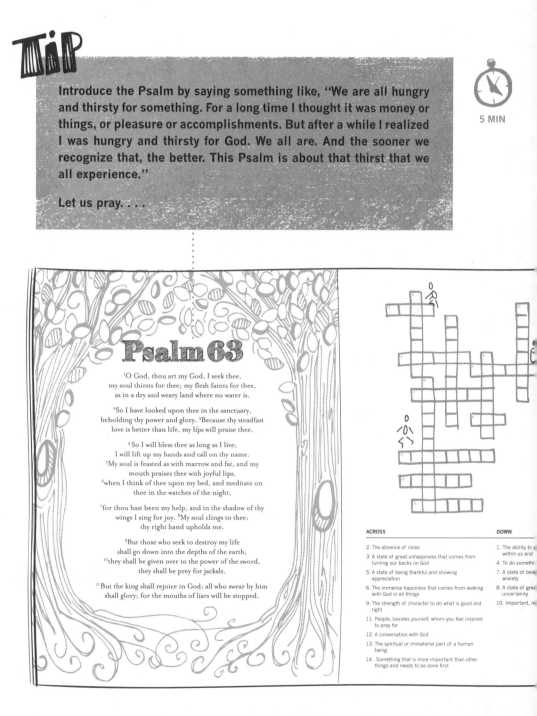

TIP

5 MIN

Introduce the Psalm by saying something like, "We are all hungry and thirsty for something. For a long time I thought it was money or things, or pleasure or accomplishments. But after a while I realized I was hungry and thirsty for God. We all are. And the sooner we recognize that, the better. This Psalm is about that thirst that we all experience."

Let us pray. . . .

Psalm 63

¹O God, thou art my God, I seek thee,
my soul thirsts for thee; my flesh faints for thee,
as in a dry and weary land where no water is.

²So I have looked upon thee in the sanctuary,
beholding thy power and glory. ³Because thy steadfast
love is better than life, my lips will praise thee.

⁴So I will bless thee as long as I live;
I will lift up my hands and call on thy name.
⁵My soul is feasted as with marrow and fat, and my
mouth praises thee with joyful lips,
⁶when I think of thee upon my bed, and meditate on
thee in the watches of the night;

⁷for thou hast been my help, and in the shadow of thy
wings I sing for joy. ⁸My soul clings to thee;
thy right hand upholds me.

⁹But those who seek to destroy my life
shall go down into the depths of the earth;
¹⁰they shall be given over to the power of the sword,
they shall be prey for jackals.

¹¹But the king shall rejoice in God; all who swear by him
shall glory; for the mouths of liars will be stopped.

ACROSS

2. The absence of noise
3. A state of great unhappiness that comes from turning our backs on God
5. A state of being thankful and showing appreciation
6. The immense happiness that comes from walking with God in all things
9. The strength of character to do what is good and right
11. People, besides yourself, whom you feel inspired to pray for
12. A conversation with God
13. The spiritual or immaterial part of a human being
14. Something that is more important than other things and needs to be done first

DOWN

1. The ability to g[...] within us and [...]
4. To do somethi[...]
7. A state of bei[...] anxiety
8. A state of grea[...] uncertainty
10. Important, n[...]

The BIBLE

Loving Father, Thank you for this day and thank you for this opportunity to explore your Word in the Scriptures. Inspire me to live with passion and purpose. Help me to discover the genius of your ways. Quiet my mind and open my heart so that I can hear exactly what you are trying to say to me today. Give me wisdom to embrace your ways with joy; give me courage to walk with you at every moment; give me strength when the world makes me weary; and help me to remember that I can always find rest and renewal in the Scriptures. Amen.

Matthew Kelly

QUICK SESSION OVERVIEW

STEP 1 WELCOME

STEP 2 OPENING PRAYER

STEP 3 ENGAGE – WATCH & DISCUSS

STEP 4 JOURNAL

STEP 5 ANNOUNCEMENTS

STEP 6 CLOSING PRAYER

SESSION FIVE: THE BIBLE

Objectives:

- To give candidates a general introduction to the Bible.

- To demonstrate that the Word of God is a practical and powerful source of inspiration and direction in our lives.

- To encourage candidates to develop the habit of reading the Bible regularly.

STEP 1 WELCOME ···

How welcome are you making your candidates feel? Greet them at the door. Have you learned their names? Greeting them by name is powerful; it shows they matter. It's just one of a hundred ways you can show them that you care.

How into it are you? They can tell. Get into it. If you don't feel like you are into it enough, spend some more time preparing for each session. Preparation breeds confidence.

✳ LEADER GUIDE KEY

TIME-ICON: This icon serves as a guide to help you plan approximately how long each activity will take.

[WB5] This code serves as a reference to point you to the page in the Workbook where you can find the related activity/content.

Example: **[WB5]** *points you to page 5 in the Workbook*

The flag icon is the halfway mark and suggests a good breaking point if your program runs twenty-four classes (or approximately 60 minutes) instead of twelve 120 minute classes.

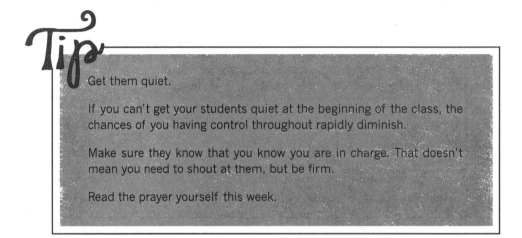

Get them quiet.

If you can't get your students quiet at the beginning of the class, the chances of you having control throughout rapidly diminish.

Make sure they know that you know you are in charge. That doesn't mean you need to shout at them, but be firm.

Read the prayer yourself this week.

2 MIN

Loving Father, Thank you for this day and thank you for this opportunity to explore your Word in the Scriptures. Inspire me to live with passion and purpose. Help me to discover the genius of your ways. Quiet my mind and open my heart so that I can hear exactly what you are trying to say to me today. Give me wisdom to embrace your ways with joy; give me courage to walk with you at every moment; give me strength when the world makes me weary; and help me to remember that I can always find rest and renewal in the Scriptures. Amen.

— *Matthew Kelly* —

STEP 3 ENGAGE: WATCH & DISCUSS

SESSION 5 INTRODUCTION

WATCH VIDEO

13 MIN

TIP: This short film is a little longer than the rest. You may want to prepare them for that, so they know what to expect. You may also want to tell them the question you are going to ask them at the end of the film. It is always the same for the first film in each session: What is the one idea in this short film that you found most helpful?

DISCUSSION QUESTION

1) What is the one idea in this short film that you found most helpful?

3 MIN

SESSION 5.1 A MAP FOR THE JOURNEY

WATCH VIDEO

7 MIN

5.1 A Map for the Journey

DISCUSSION QUESTIONS [WB115]

10 MIN

Tip This section talks about the Bible as a map and guidebook. You may want to share a personal story about how the Bible was a map for you at some point in your life. The more specific your testimony can be, the more powerful it will be.

1) Do you think of the Bible as a guidebook? If not what is your perception of the Bible?

2) In what ways are you a tourist and in what ways are you a pilgrim?

3) How comfortable would you be if you died today and had to account for the way you have lived your life?

EXERCISE

5 MIN

Invite a student to read **"Who Was Saint Jerome?"** Ask the candidates what they think it would be like to copy the whole Bible in their own handwriting, or to translate it into another language. [WB126]

TIP!

Eye contact is key. When you are speaking to them, look them in the eye. Resist the temptation to bury your head in this leader guide. Look up; look them in the eye, especially when they are responding to a question.

TRUE GOD FROM TRUE GOD, BEGOTTEN, NOT MADE, CONSUBSTANTIAL WITH THE FATHER; THROUGH HIM ALL THINGS WERE MADE. FOR US MEN AND FOR OUR SALVATION HE CAME DOWN FROM HEAVEN, AND BY THE

"GOOD, BETTER, BEST. NEVER LET IT REST. TILL YOUR GOOD IS BETTER AND YOUR BETTER IS BEST."

SAINT JEROME

SAINT JEROME (347-420) was a priest, confessor, theologian, and historian. He is most famous for translating the Bible into Latin. It took him twenty-three years to complete the translation. Can you imagine translating the whole Bible? Jerome wrote,

"IGNORANCE OF SCRIPTURES IS IGNORANCE OF CHRIST."

He is the patron saint of librarians and his feast day is September 30.

Prayer Process, it is important that you don't just sit there and think about it. The point is to have a conversation with God about whatever that particular Scripture stirs in your heart.

Another great way to connect with the Scriptures is to bring your Bible to Mass. Sure, most churches have those booklets that have the readings in them, but there is something very powerful about holding a Bible. It's different. Try it and you will see.

This requires some advance preparation. I like to mark the readings with Post-it notes before I go to Mass. Otherwise, I am distracted looking for the readings in my Bible during Mass. Next week's readings are usually published in the bulletin, or you can find them online.

Spend some time preparing for Mass next week, and bring your Bible—you will have a completely different experience.

I also want to encourage you to bring your Bible to these classes. Throughout the rest of this program we will be referring to passages from the Bible. Each time we do, find the passage in your Bible and mark it with an asterisk or underline it.

Don't be afraid to write in your Bible. It's yours. It's there to help you learn and grow spiritually, and sometimes highlighting a passage or underlining a phrase can be very helpful. This will also help you over time to see what parts of the Bible you have spent time with.

The last thing I want to encourage you to do in this section is to identify some favorite Bible passages. Memorize them. These will be of great comfort and guidance to you throughout your life.

Here are some of mine:

"Be still and know that I am God." Psalm 46:10

Life is busy and noisy and distracting, and that can all be overwhelming at times. Sometimes it helps just to sit down, be quiet, sit still, and recognize God's presence.

Another of my favorite Scripture passages is:

"Seek first the kingdom of God and his justice, and all else will be given in addition." Matthew 6:33

You will be amazed the clarity that this one line of Scripture can bring to decision-making. We are making hundreds of choices every day, and each choice celebrates the kingdom of God or rejects it. Happiness comes from seeking God and his kingdom. If we put that first in our decisions, so many of the other things of this world will take care of themselves.

"What does the Lord require of you? But to live justly, love tenderly, and to walk humbly with your God." Micah 6:8

This is almost like a mini-Gospel. We could spend our whole lives just reflecting on this one passage, examining ourselves each day: Am I living justly? Am I loving tenderly? Am I walking humbly with my God?

Finally, I would like to encourage you to have a favorite Psalm. Read it often, but also memorize it. There will be times in your life when you are too tired, too distracted, or too conflicted to form your own words for prayer. At these times you will find yourself praying your Psalm.

My favorite is Psalm 23: *"The Lord is my shepherd, there is nothing I shall want. . . ."*

There are a hundred ways to invite the Scriptures into our lives. I hope you will make reading the Bible part of your daily routine. If you do, I am confident you will find it a life-changing habit.

What do you think Mary looked forward to each day?

IF YOU DON'T HAVE TIME TO PRAY AND READ THE SCRIPTURES, YOU ARE BUSIER THAN GOD EVER INTENDED YOU TO BE.

SESSION 5.2 INTRODUCTION TO THE BIBLE

WATCH VIDEO

7 MIN

Before you start this short film, ask them how many books are in the Bible. See if the class knows or can agree. Don't answer the question; let the short film answer it.

DISCUSSION QUESTIONS [WB121]

10 MIN

1) What new thing did you learn about the Bible in this section?

2) What's your favorite book in the Bible? Why?

3) If you could be one person in the Bible, who would you want to be? Why?

SESSION 5.3 HOW SHOULD I USE THE BIBLE?

WATCH VIDEO

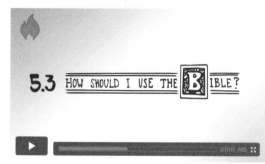

9 MIN

TIP

Feel free to walk around during the discussions. This will help to hold their attention. If someone is speaking, move a little closer to them. This helps them to know that you are curious and interested in what they have to say. If someone is not on task or is misbehaving, move closer to them. This proximity control is a good nonverbal way to capture attention.

DISCUSSION QUESTIONS [WB128]

10 MIN

1) How do you feel about the challenge to read the Bible for a few minutes each day?

2) How do you think your life would change if you did read the Bible for a few minutes each day?

3) Other than reading the Bible, what other habits could help you become the-best-version-of-yourself?

STEP 3 ENGAGE: WATCH & DISCUSS

CONTINUED...

5 MIN

EXERCISE: **TOP TEN CATHOLIC PILGRIMAGES**

Ask someone to read aloud "Top Ten Catholic Pilgrimages." Next, invite students to write down quietly which of the ten they would most like to visit and why. Now go around the class and ask each student which they selected. Finally, ask if anyone has been to any of these places. If there is time, invite them to share about their experiences. [WB113]

Tip

If your group is too large for everyone to share, just ask them to select a partner and share their answer with that partner.

I BELIEVE IN ONE, HOLY, CATHOLIC AND APOSTOLIC CHURCH. I CONFESS ONE BAPTISM FOR THE FORGIVE

5. THE BIBLE

Albert Einstein said, "I want to know the thoughts of God, the rest are details."

The Bible is not just another book. It's the Word of God. You have probably heard that a lot. But what does it really mean? For one thing, words have value based on who speaks them. If you knew someone who was always telling lies and he told you something, you would discount what he said because you know from experience that he has a habit of lying.

Some people's words should be discounted. But this here—the Bible, the Word of God—is not to be discounted. God should be taken at his word. The Bible should be taken very seriously. Your happiness in this life and the next life depends in large part on how seriously you take the Word of God.

Here's the mysterious thing about the Bible: It has the power to transform our lives. That's why so many people don't read it! Seriously.

God wants to transform you and your life. Too often when we pray, we pray for tweaking. We want God to tweak this and tweak that. But God is not interested in tweaking. God is in the business of transformation. He wants to turn your life upside down, which as it turns out is right side up. He wants to transform the way you think about yourself, he wants to transform the way you think about relationships, he wants to transform the way you think about money and career, and he wants to transform the way you think about the world and the culture.

If you want to see something incredible, start praying for transformation. Ask God to transform you and your life. Most people have never prayed a prayer of transformation.

The truth is, your happiness depends upon discovering God's will for your life, and the Bible can help you with that. But too often we are not interested in discovering the will of God. Usually we are more interested in "my will be done" than "thy will be done." Think about it: When was the last time you actively sought out God's will in a situation?

The Bible leads us to God's mysterious and fabulous plan for our lives—and that is always transformational. This is not just another book.

—Albert Einstien—

○○**START**○○
praying for
TRANSFORMATION
○○○○○○○○○○

5.1 A Map for the Journey

→ WHAT IS A ←

PILGRIMAGE?

A spiritual journey to a holy place.

Many years ago, I read an article in a travel magazine about the Camino. The Camino is a pilgrimage, a five-hundred-mile walk that begins in the South of France, crosses the Pyrenees into Spain, and then works its way across northern Spain, finishing in Santiago de Compostela—where Saint James, one of the twelve apostles, is buried.

I remember reading the article and thinking that it would be an amazing adventure . . . but I also remember thinking that it was the kind of thing that I would never do. Why? Two main reasons: I am not really the outdoors type and I didn't figure I would ever take a month off. But ten years later, I decided to make the pilgrimage.

A pilgrimage is a spiritual journey to a holy place. Sometimes people go on a pilgrimage in search of answers to questions, and sometimes they do it to thank God for a special favor. I was going for both reasons. I was grateful for all the blessings God had given me, but I had questions about what I should do with the rest of my life.

I blocked a whole month on my schedule (a year in advance) and began to research everything I needed to know for the trip. I read books, studied the route, looked into where to eat and where to stay along the way, what the weather would be like, what clothes to bring and what boots to wear, what to pack and what to leave behind, and I talked to people who had made the journey.

My biggest question was: How will I know if I am going the right way? I had read that an image of a seashell was used to direct pilgrims along the path. But I had also heard that in many places this symbol was faded, which often caused pilgrims to take the wrong path.

Then, I met a couple who had made the pilgrimage seven times. They said to me, "You've got to get a copy of this particular guidebook! It's the bible of the Camino." I immediately ordered a copy.

The book was amazing. It had maps and routes, suggested starting and ending points for each day, elevations and distances. It showed you where fresh water was available to fill your water bottle, and warned you not to drink the water in certain places. It showed you options for where to stay and where to eat. It marked spots on the map where the signs were faded, and gave specific instructions about what to do in those places. And at every step along the way, it told you how far to the next place for food, water, or sleep. That guidebook was invaluable. It gave me confidence for the journey.

The Bible is that guidebook for your life.

TOP TEN CATHOLIC PILGRIMAGES

1. St. Peter's Basilica, the Vatican
2. Jerusalem, Israel
3. Lourdes, France
4. Fatima, Portugal
5. Camino de Santiago, Spain
6. Ephesus, Greece
7. Guadalupe, Mexico
8. Czestochowa, Poland
9. Assisi, Italy
10. Knock, Ireland

"A thorough knowledge of the Bible is worth more than a college education.

THEODORE ROOSEVELT

WATCH VIDEO

Tell them that this short film is about the most powerful thing in their lives.

7 MIN

DISCUSSION QUESTIONS [WB133]

1) Who do you know who has great habits? What are those habits?

2) Have you ever seen bad habits destroy a person's life?

3) What will be the biggest obstacle to you establishing the habit of reading the Bible for a few minutes each day?

10 MIN

EXERCISE VIRTUE IN FOCUS

5 MIN

This session highlights the virtue of kindness. Invite a candidate to read aloud the **Virtue in Focus** section. Choose one of the questions from the section and encourage the candidates to share their answers. [WB130]

AND BY THE HOLY SPIRIT WAS INCARNATE OF THE VIRGIN MARY, AND BECAME MAN. FOR OUR SAKE HE WAS CRUCIFIED UNDER PONTIUS PILATE, HE SUFFERED DEATH AND WAS B

VIRTUE IN FOCUS

Kind·ness
[kahynd·nis]

The act of being friendly, generous, and considerate.

Has anyone shown you kindness today? Who? How?

How does it make you feel when someone is kind to you?

Who is one person in your life whom God is calling you to be kinder to?

5.4 THE POWER OF HABIT

Albert Einstein also said, "Compound interest is the most powerful force in the universe." You might be thinking, what on earth does compound interest have to do with the Bible. Let me explain.

To demonstrate the power of compound interest, let's take a look at an example.

If from your eighteenth birthday you saved just three dollars a day, every day, until your sixty-fifth birthday, you would have saved $51,465. But if you invested that money at a compounding interest rate of 10 percent, you would have more than a million dollars—$1,017,046, to be exact.

But most people don't retire with anywhere near that much money. In fact, the latest data shows that at age sixty-five the average American has a net worth of just $66,740. Most people never engage the power of compounding interest. Most wait until far too late in life to start saving for retirement—and it matters.

In the example we discussed, if everything else remained the same except you waited until you were thirty to start saving your three dollars a day, instead of retiring with more than a million dollars, you would have just $316,115.

What's the lesson here? The earlier you start saving the better.

Habits are even more powerful than compounding interest, and they have the same powerful compounding impact on our lives. The earlier you develop some foundational positive habits, the better.

What are your habits? What are the things you do every day or every week with unrelenting consistency? Are they helping you or hurting you?

Tell me what your habits are and I will tell you what your future looks like. Thoughts become choices, choices become actions, actions become habits, habits become character, and your character is your destiny. Your life is running in the direction of your habits much faster than you might think.

Life is choices. Make a choice often enough and it will become an ingrained habit.

You can, of course, be on the wrong side of compound interest. Run up some credit card debt that you can't pay off and you will discover

that many of those cards have 21 percent interest rates. You will then find yourself very much on the wrong side of compounding interest.

The same can happen with habits. No drug addict or alcoholic ever set out to become a slave to their addiction. It happened one step at a time, one choice at a time, and before they knew it they were trapped. Habits are incredibly powerful—for better or for worse.

How would you like your life to be different this year than it was last year? Our lives change when our habits change. If you want your life to be different this year, change your habits. If you want to do better academically, change your habits. If you want to do better in a sport, change your habits. If you want to have more fulfilling relationships, change your habits.

You may be quite content with your life today, but there will be times when you will encounter profound discontentment. When you come to those moments, I want you to remember: Our lives change when our habits change.

Throughout this program I am trying to help you to establish some foundational habits in your life. In Session 4 we explored the habit of daily prayer. Now I want to encourage you to add the habit of reading the Bible for a few minutes each day. Perhaps you could start your day reading a chapter from the Bible and end your day with The Prayer Process. There are going to be a few defining foundational habits in your life. I hope prayer and reading the Bible are among them.

There are so many habits, good and bad, that can impact the direction of your life. You know the habits that will help you become the-best-version-of-yourself and the ones that will not.

What will be the defining habits of your life?

Let me share with you something I have learned from trying to read the Bible each day for twenty years: It is never convenient. It is always inconvenient. There are always other things you could be doing, and often there will be other things you would rather be doing. There will be those days when you yearn to read the Bible and talk with God about what you discover. But those days will likely be quite rare. There are going to be times when you feel like you are getting nothing out of it. When you encounter those times I want to encourage you to persevere. At those times I want you to hear me whispering into your ear, "Press on. Press on. The effort will be worth it in the long run."

One day you will be glad you did. I promise you.

WATCH VIDEO

Tip

Do you know everyone's name yet? If not, learn them. If you know them, use them.

3 MIN

EXERCISE: Know It. Think About It. Live It.

TIP

How many Bibles are in the room today? Count them. Congratulate someone who brought his or her Bible for the first time. Ask a candidate to look up the passage highlighted in the section **KNOW IT. THINK ABOUT IT. LIVE IT.** Ask another student to read the text from the workbook. [WB124]

3 MIN

OF ALL THINGS VISIBLE AND INVISIBLE. I BELIEVE IN ONE LORD JESUS CHRIST, THE ONLY BEGOTTEN SON OF GOD, BORN OF THE FATHER BEFORE ALL AGES. GOD FROM GOD, LIGHT FROM LIGHT, TRUE GOD FROM TR

5.3 HOW SHOULD I USE THE 📖 BIBLE?

When it comes to reading the Bible, the first rule is: Don't be intimidated. So many people never read the Bible because they get intimidated. If you come across something you don't understand, just press on. Don't get bogged down.

Don't be intimidated by the Bible. This is our book. It lays out a blueprint for happiness. It helps us to know the heart of God, and his incredible dreams for us. And the Bible teaches us how to listen to the voice of God in our own lives.

So, where to start?

I would like to recommend that you start with three books.

1. The Gospel of Matthew.

First, as we discussed in Session 3, read the Gospel of Matthew. This will help you to delve deeply into the life and teachings of Jesus.

2. The book of Genesis.

Next read Genesis. This will give you incredible insight into the human condition, show you what happens when we walk with God and what happens when we turn our backs on him, and help you to see that the world is a bit of a mess and the Gospel is the antidote.

3. The book of Psalms.

Finally, read the Psalms, better still—pray them! This is the most beautiful collection of prayers. Here you will find a prayer for every occasion in your life. You will encounter every emotion in the Psalms: joy, sorrow, hope, desperation, trust, fear, confusion, clarity, and many more.

Begin by reading one chapter a day. It will take you twenty-eight days to work your way through Matthew and fifty days to make your journey through Genesis. If you then pray three Psalms a day it will take you fifty days to make your way through all 150 Psalms.

In just 128 days you will have a good sense of what the Bible is all about.

"LOOK, THE VIRGIN SHALL CONCEIVE AND BEAR A SON, AND THEY SHALL NAME HIM EMMANUEL, WHICH MEANS 'GOD IS WITH US.'"
Matthew 1:23

KNOW IT: At every moment of every day God is with us.

THINK ABOUT IT: Do you recognize and acknowledge Gods presence in your daily life? Or are you oblivious to him by your side?

LIVE IT: Today when you are moving from one activity to another, use those gaps in your day to talk to God about what just happened of what is about to happen.

When you read your chapter, approach it with an open heart, listening for what God is saying to you. As you read, identify a word, phrase, or idea in each chapter that jumps out at you, something that taps you on the shoulder.

For example, you might be reading the first chapter of Matthew's Gospel. The first seventeen verses are the genealogy of Jesus—not the most interesting piece of Bible for a Bible rookie. But the phrase that often strikes me when I read this first chapter of Matthew is verse 23: "Look, the virgin shall conceive and bear a son, and they shall name him Emmanuel, which means 'God is with us.'"

"God is with us." There may have been times in your life when God has felt very far away. There have been almost certainly been times when you have wandered far from God. I hope there have also been some times in your life when you have felt God was near. But here is the elemental truth: God is with us.

And each day, before you begin reading the Bible, pray asking God to help you to listen to what he is trying to say to you. It could be something as a simple as:

"Loving Father, I know you have good plans for me. Open my heart and my mind so that I can hear clearly what you are trying to say to me through the Scriptures today."

The process is quite simple.

1. Begin with a short prayer.

2. Read a chapter of the Bible.

3. Pick out a word, phrase, or idea that jumps out at you.

4. Talk to God about it.

If you read the same chapter many times, you might be drawn to different phrases or ideas on different days.

Even if you pick the same phrase, you may have very different conversations with God about that same phrase. Perhaps you pick the phrase "God is with us." You may have a conversation with God about how you sense his presence guiding you and encouraging you. But you may come back in a couple of years and read the same chapter, pick out the same phrase, and have a conversation with God about how he feels far from you at that time.

Talk to God about the word or phrase that strikes you, and listen for what he is trying to say to you through it. Just as we discussed with The

THE PROCESS IS QUITE SIMPLE.

① Begin with a short prayer.

② Read a chapter of the Bible.

③ Pick out a word, phrase or idea that jumps out at you.

④ Talk to God about it.

124 | **DECISION POINT**

THE BIBLE | 125

STEP 4 JOURNAL

5 MIN

INSTRUCTIONS: It's time to journal. Remind them that this is a sacred time. Invite your class to open up to page 137 and take a few minutes in silence to journal their answers to those questions.

TIP

Talk about how busy your life is and how you have to fight and make it a priority to have any quiet time. Let them know that this time to think, pray, and journal is a real luxury.

STEP 5 ANNOUNCEMENTS

2 MIN

Tip

Smile. Thank them for coming. Remind them you will be praying for them during the week. Ask them if there is anything in particular they would like you to pray for. Tell them that if it is private they can write it down and pass it to you.

Think about getting a prayer book that your students can write their intentions in. Tell them you will take the prayer book home with you and pray for their needs and intentions. You will get incredible insight into their lives by doing this.

STEP 6 · CLOSING PRAYER ·

TIP

4 MIN

Invite the class to settle down. Get still and quiet. Allow them just to be in that stillness and quiet for a few seconds. Encourage them to take a few deep breaths and to listen to the Psalm.

After the Psalm, close with a spontaneous prayer inviting God to pour out his grace and guidance on these young people between now and the next time you are all together.

Let us pray. . . .

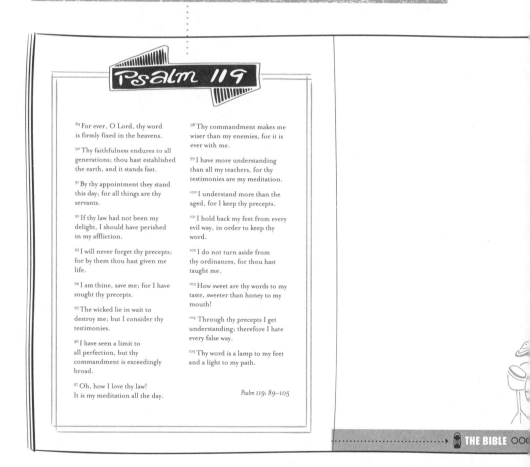

Psalm 119

[89] For ever, O Lord, thy word is firmly fixed in the heavens.

[90] Thy faithfulness endures to all generations; thou hast established the earth, and it stands fast.

[91] By thy appointment they stand this day; for all things are thy servants.

[92] If thy law had not been my delight, I should have perished in my affliction.

[93] I will never forget thy precepts; for by them thou hast given me life.

[94] I am thine, save me; for I have sought thy precepts.

[95] The wicked lie in wait to destroy me; but I consider thy testimonies.

[96] I have seen a limit to all perfection, but thy commandment is exceedingly broad.

[97] Oh, how I love thy law! It is my meditation all the day.

[98] Thy commandment makes me wiser than my enemies, for it is ever with me.

[99] I have more understanding than all my teachers, for thy testimonies are my meditation.

[100] I understand more than the aged, for I keep thy precepts.

[101] I hold back my feet from every evil way, in order to keep thy word.

[102] I do not turn aside from thy ordinances, for thou hast taught me.

[103] How sweet are thy words to my taste, sweeter than honey to my mouth!

[104] Through thy precepts I get understanding; therefore I hate every false way.

[105] Thy word is a lamp to my feet and a light to my path.

Psalm 119: 89–105

RELATIONSHIPS

Lord of all pots and pans and things, since I've no time to be a great saint by doing lovely things, or watching late with thee, or dreaming in the dawnlight, or storming heaven's gates, make me a saint by getting meals, and washing up the plates. Warm all the kitchen with thy love, and light it with thy peace; forgive me all my worrying, and make my grumbling cease. Thou who didst love to give men food, in room, or by the sea, accept the service that I do, I do it unto thee. Amen.

— Brother Lawrence —

QUICK SESSION OVERVIEW

STEP 1 **WELCOME**
STEP 2 **OPENING PRAYER**
STEP 3 **ENGAGE – WATCH & DISCUSS**
STEP 4 **JOURNAL**
STEP 5 **ANNOUNCEMENTS**
STEP 6 **CLOSING PRAYER**

SESSION SIX: RELATIONSHIPS

Objectives:

- Establish the purpose of relationships and that the most important relationship in our lives is with God.

- Teach candidates how to make good decisions in the area of relationships.

- Demonstrate that developing healthy relationships is essential to the life God is calling us to live.

Mix it up. Have some great Christian music playing when your class arrives. When everyone has arrived and is settled, invite them to listen quietly to one particular song. Ask them to listen and then write down their reactions to the song.

Remember: Smile. Welcome them. Make them feel special. Let your excitement for the possibilities before them overflow.

LEADER GUIDE KEY

TIME-ICON: This icon serves as a guide to help you plan approximately how long each activity will take.

[WB5] This code serves as a reference to point you to the page in the Workbook where you can find the related activity/content.

Example: **[WB5]** *points you to page 5 in the Workbook*

The flag icon is the halfway mark and suggests a good breaking point if your program runs twenty-four classes (or approximately 60 minutes) instead of twelve 120 minute classes.

Tip

It's time to get quiet and pray together. The prayer for this session is about doing the ordinary things of everyday life with great love, and thus transforming them into a great prayer.

Talk to them about some of the everyday things you have to do that you would rather not. Tell them how offering these tasks to God is one of the ways that our faith is very practical. Talk about how this helps you stay focused every day on becoming the-best-version-of-yourself.

Now read the prayer slowly and deliberately.

3 MIN

Lord of all pots and pans and things, since I've no time to be a great saint by doing lovely things, or watching late with thee, or dreaming in the dawnlight, or storming heaven's gates, make me a saint by getting meals, and washing up the plates. Warm all the kitchen with thy love, and light it with thy peace; forgive me all my worrying, and make my grumbling cease. Thou who didst love to give men food, in room, or by the sea, accept the service that I do, I do it unto thee. Amen.

· —— *Brother Lawrence* —— ·

STEP 3 ENGAGE: WATCH & DISCUSS

SESSION 6 INTRODUCTION

WATCH VIDEO

4 MIN

Speak up. They can tell by the strength of your voice how confident you are. Everything you have to say is worth hearing. They need to hear these things, even though they may not want to hear them. So speak up. Make yourself heard.

DISCUSSION QUESTION

1) What is the one idea in this short film that you found most helpful?

4 MIN

SESSION 6.1 **WHAT IS THE PURPOSE?**

WATCH VIDEO

8 MIN

10 MIN

DISCUSSION QUESTIONS [WB145]

Tip   Understanding anything begins with exploring and discovering its purpose. Imagine trying to play football or volleyball without a clear understanding of the game's purpose. Purpose is essential. In this section we are going to explore the purpose of relationships. This is life-changing stuff—remind them of that.

1) Who are the most important people in your life? Why?

2) What is the purpose of relationships?

3) What are you pretending to not know about your approach to relationships?

EXERCISE

Invite a student to read aloud **"Who Was John the Apostle?"** Ask the class, "How good a friend are you to Jesus?" Ask them to give themselves a score between one and ten. [WB142]

TIP! Don't let up on the Jesus thing. We don't talk anywhere near enough about friendship with Jesus. Keep coming back to this. If we can help them develop this friendship with Jesus, a lot of other things will just fall into place.

HE ASCENDED INTO HEAVEN AND IS SEATED AT THE RIGHT HAND OF THE FATHER. HE WILL COME AGAIN IN GLORY TO JUDGE THE LIVING AND THE DEAD AND HIS KINGDOM WILL HAVE NO END. I BELIEVE IN THE HOL

6. RELATIONSHIPS

My father died of cancer when I was thirty. It was very painful, but I have many great memories of him. He was a wise and patient man who always had practical insights into the situations of my life. I often find myself thinking about some of the unforgettable conversations we had. One of those conversations was about friendship.

One Saturday we were watching one of my brothers play soccer, and the stands were quite empty. Dad asked me how things were going at school and I was telling him about some problems I was having with a friend.

I remember as if it happened yesterday: He turned to me, held up his hand, stretched out his fingers, and said, "Matthew, true friendship is rare. Much rarer than most people think. If you find five true friends in this life you will be a very blessed man."

At the time I thought to myself, "Five! I've got tons of friends." But as time has passed, life has revealed the wisdom in my father's words. True friendship is incredibly rare.

We all need a few great friends to do life with. We need friends who will challenge us when we need to be challenged, encourage us when we need to be encouraged, and be genuinely happy for us when we succeed. We all need a handful of friends who can help us to become the-best-version-of-ourselves.

Finding that handful of friends is not just going to happen. It requires patience, self-control, trust, and some great decisions. God wants to help you to develop fabulous relationships.

The truth is, a great deal of your happiness and a great deal of your misery in this life will probably come from relationships—so it is important to get this right!

6.1 WHAT IS THE PURPOSE?

Developing great relationships is like constructing a great building. The first stage is design, and design is driven by purpose. The best warehouse in the world would not serve very well as a family home, and the best family home in the world would not serve very well as a warehouse.

Everything has a purpose. If you want to succeed at something, the first thing you need to get really clear about is purpose. The purpose of golf is to shoot your lowest possible score, the purpose of football is to score more points than the other team, the purpose of business is to be profitable by adding value to your customers' lives so that they will continue to purchase your products and services, and the ultimate purpose of life is to get to Heaven.

But what is the purpose of relationships?

The sad thing is, too many people never really explore this question. As a result, when we look around society today we don't see too many dynamic and healthy relationships.

Lots of people think the purpose of relationships is just to have fun. Relationships should be fun, but they are not going to be fun all the time, and fun is not the main purpose. If you think it is, you will fail in relationships.

So, what is the purpose of relationships?

To answer this question, we must first revisit the purpose of life.

We have already spoken about God's dream for us to become the-best-version-of-ourselves. Everything makes sense in relation to God's dream for us—including relationships. In our discussion of the Bible we talked about being pilgrims. This world is not our final destination; we are just passing through here. We have talked time and time again about God's overwhelming desire for a relationship with us. God wants us to walk with him in this life and be with him for eternity in Heaven.

God gives us relationships to help us become the-best-version-of-ourselves. He gives us relationships so that we can help each other get to Heaven.

My number one job in my marriage is to help my wife Meggie get to Heaven. My number one job as a parent is to help my kids to know and love God and get to Heaven. My number one job as a friend is to help my friends get to Heaven. So each day I encourage my wife, my children, and my friends to become a-better-version-of-themselves. Why? Because it is impossible to grow in virtue and character and not draw nearer to God. It is impossible to become a-better-version-of-yourself and not be one step closer to Heaven.

The purpose of every relationship is two people helping each other become the-best-version-of-themselves. It doesn't matter if a relationship is between husband and wife, boyfriend and girlfriend, brother and sister, parents and children, manager and employee, coach and player, teacher and student. The purpose of every relationship is to help each other become the-best-version-of-ourselves. I am here to help you become the-best-version-of-yourself, and you are here to help me become the-best-version-of-myself.

WHO WAS JOHN the APOSTLE?

Saint John the Apostle (AD 6–100) was one of the Twelve Apostles of Jesus. He was also the brother of James. The Church Fathers generally identify him as the author of five books of the Bible: the Gospel of John, three epistles of John, and the book of Revelation. He was the only male follower of Jesus at the foot of the cross with Mary. How many of your friends would stay with you as John stayed with Jesus? John is the patron saint of friendship and his feast day is January 20.

YOU WILL LEARN MORE FROM YOUR FRIENDS THAN YOU EVER WILL FROM BOOKS. CHOOSE YOUR FRIENDS WISELY.

SESSION 6.2 CHOOSE YOUR FRIENDS WISELY

WATCH VIDEO

9 MIN

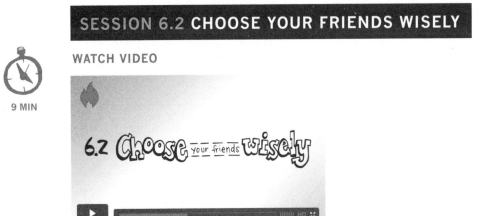

6.2 Choose your friends wisely

T I P Check in. Ask them how this is going. Explore with them how this experience is different from what they expected when they began the journey toward Confirmation.

DISCUSSION QUESTIONS [WB151]

10 MIN

1) What is the best friendship decision you have made in the last twelve months?

2) How do you feel God is calling you to improve the relationship with your parents?

3) Are your friends helping you to become the-best-version-of-yourself? Are you helping them to become the-best-version-of-themselves?

SESSION 6.3 WHAT IS LOVE?

WATCH VIDEO

9 MIN

Before you start this short film, ask them what the most important relationship is in their lives. Ask them how it has changed over the years. As an example, remind them that when they were infants they couldn't do anything without their mother, and at that time their relationship with their mother was the most important in their lives.

DISCUSSION QUESTIONS [WB157]

10 MIN

1) What did you learn about love in this session?

2) Who models selfless love in your life?

3) How does your relationship with God influence your relationships with other people?

STEP 3 **ENGAGE: WATCH & DISCUSS**
CONTINUED...

EXERCISE:
CROSSWORD PUZZLE · · · · · · · · · · ·

5 MIN

Tip

Ask each candidate to find a partner and do the crossword together. Make it fun. Have a contest to see which pair finishes first. [WB164]

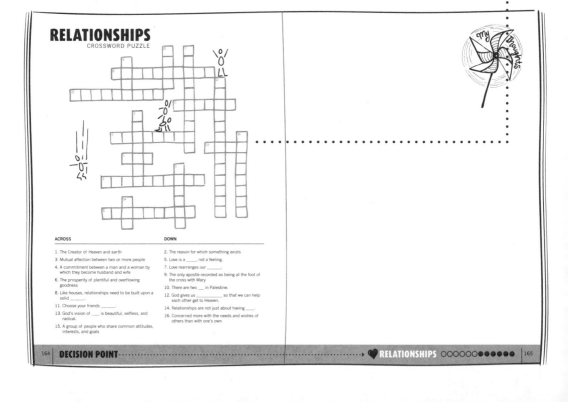

RELATIONSHIPS
CROSSWORD PUZZLE

ACROSS

1. The Creator of Heaven and earth
3. Mutual affection between two or more people
4. A commitment between a man and a woman by which they become husband and wife
6. The prosperity of plentiful and overflowing goodness
8. Like houses, relationships need to be built upon a solid _____.
11. Choose your friends _____.
13. God's vision of ___ is beautiful, selfless, and radical.
15. A group of people who share common attitudes, interests, and goals

DOWN

2. The reason for which something exists
5. Love is a _____, not a feeling.
7. Love rearranges our _____.
9. The only apostle recorded as being at the foot of the cross with Mary
10. There are two ___ in Palestine.
12. God gives us _____ so that we can help each other get to Heaven.
14. Relationships are not just about having ___.
16. Concerned more with the needs and wishes of others than with one's own

SESSION 6.4 YOUR QUEST FOR LOVE

WATCH VIDEO

Tell them that the last two sentences in this short film contain one of the best messages in the whole program.

5 MIN

DISCUSSION QUESTIONS [WB160]

1) In what ways have you gone looking for love in the wrong places?

10 MIN

2) Who do you know who has a great marriage? What do you admire about their marriage?

3) What virtue do you think is most important to healthy relationships?

EXERCISE VIRTUE IN FOCUS

5 MIN

TIP

This session highlights the virtue of goodness. Invite a candidate to read aloud the **Virtue in Focus** section. Choose one of the questions from the section and encourage the candidates to share their answers. [WB149]

6.2 Choose your friends wisely

Many of the most important decisions you will make in your life will be around relationships. Here are five examples:

1. FRIENDS. The friends you choose to surround yourself with now and throughout your life will have an enormous impact. Sooner or later, we all rise or fall to the level of our friendships. If your friends take their studies seriously, chances are you will too. If your friends get into drugs and alcohol, chances are you will also. If your friends waste endless hours sitting around playing video games, chances are you will too. Friends are a powerful habit, for better or for worse. Are your friends helping you become the-best-version-of-yourself? Are you helping them to become-the-best-version-of-themselves?

You are going to make a lot of friendship decisions throughout your life. Get into the habit now of asking the Holy Spirit to guide your friendship decisions.

2. PARENTS. Your relationship with your parents is a central relationship in your life. It is now, and it always will be. My dad has been dead for ten years, and there are still days when I think to myself, "I should call Dad and tell him that . . ," and then I catch myself and remember he is not with us anymore. A week does not pass when I don't think about my dad and how he would advise me in a situation. Whether they are alive or not, whether you live with them or not, your bond with your parents is powerful.

This relationship is so important that it is the first human relationship to be mentioned in the Ten Commandments. The fourth commandment is: Honor your father and your mother. I heard a great story a couple of weeks ago that made me realize how powerfully and practically God uses his commandments to lead us to happiness and the fullness of life he desires for us.

Caitlin was fifteen years old when her parents thought it would be a good idea for her to go on a mission trip to serve the hungry and the homeless. She didn't want to go and didn't want to hear why her parents thought she should. Finally, her parents came to her one night and said, "We have prayed about it and we have a strong sense that you should go on this mission trip." That Saturday as they put her on the bus she was sobbing in anger because they were making her go. A week later, when she got back, she was happier than her parents had ever seen her. Her eyes had been opened to how difficult life is for so many, but she had also met Scott. Caitlin and Scott dated all through high school, all through college, and just three weeks ago, they got married. Her parents had a strong sense that Caitlin should be on that trip because God was inspiring them to send her.

Caitlin was resistant to her parents' guidance. Little did she know that God was working through them.

God works in powerful ways through his commandments. So next time your parents ask you to do something, or encourage you to consider something, you may want to politely and humbly say yes.

3. MARRIAGE. Some of you will become priests or enter religious life, but most of you will get married. Whom you decide to marry will have an enormous impact on your life and happiness. What criteria will you use to make that decision? Looks? Personality? Character? Looks matter to a certain extent. It is important that you be attracted to the person you marry. Personality matters more. But character matters most. Is this person committed to growing in godly character? Are you committed to growing in godly character? If not, then the truth is, sooner or later your marriage will most likely find itself in a very difficult place.

Marriage is a beautiful thing. It really is, and I didn't fully understand that until I was married. But marrying the right person for the right reasons is critical. Marriage may seem like something in the very distant future for you, but what I want you to know *now* is that the decisions you are making around relationships today will affect your marriage, no matter how far it is in the future.

4. COMMUNITY. We all need people to do life with—friends, family, and community to encourage us and challenge us. When we are young we find ourselves involved in various communities—school, parish, sports, and neighborhood. But as we get older we have to actively seek out community. Part of the genius of Catholicism is the parish community. Parish life provides a natural and powerful opportunity for us to encourage, challenge, and support each other.

I'm not going to lie to you. Some parish communities are better than others. But I want to encourage you to get involved in your parish more each year. Join the youth group, become a reader or a Eucharistic Minister, or get involved in any of the many groups and ministries that make up your parish community. You might say, "The youth group is lame at our parish!" Maybe it is. So do something about it. Get involved and make it better. It is easy to criticize from the sidelines.

Don't ask what your parish can do for you; ask what you can do for your parish. It is through service and sacrifice that we are very often led to the beautiful plan God has for our lives.

5. GOD. I put your relationship with God last on the list, but it is the most important. Unless you make your relationship with God a priority, your chances of getting the other relationship decisions right are next to zero.

VIRTUE IN FOCUS

Good·ness
[goo d-nis]

The quality of being good, having virtue, character, and moral excellence.

Are you striving for goodness?

How do you feel when you behave in ways that are good, virtuous, and morally excellent?

Who is one person in your life that models goodness for you?

SESSION 6.5 DECISION POINT

WATCH VIDEO

Tip
This is the shortest video in the program. Tell them that. Encourage them to focus.

2 MIN

EXERCISE: Know It. Think About It. Live It.

TIP

Did everyone bring a Bible to class today? If someone is consistently not bringing a Bible, you may need to be sensitive to the fact that they may not have one, or their parents may not be able to afford one.

Ask a candidate to look up the passage highlighted in the section **KNOW IT. THINK ABOUT IT. LIVE IT.** Ask another student to read the text from the workbook. [WB144]

5 MIN

BELIEVE IN THE HOLY SPIRIT, THE LORD, THE GIVER OF LIFE, WHO PROCEEDS FROM THE FATHER AND THE

Matthew 7:24-27

KNOW IT: There is a difference between the wise and the foolish.

THINK ABOUT IT: Are you building your life on a solid foundation like the wise man?

LIVE IT: What one thing can you do each day to strengthen the foundation you are building your life upon?

COMMON PURPOSE

Why do you think we know so little about Mary?

The world says that the secret to having great relationships is common interests. Common interests are good, but they are not the key to great relationships. Your interests ten years from now will most likely be very different from your interests today. Throughout our lives our interests are constantly changing and evolving. And if you build a relationship on common interests, if you make common interests the most important thing, and your interests change—the relationship will change. And it will very often fall apart.

Purpose matters. The foundation you choose to build your relationships upon matters. Think about the story from Matthew's Gospel. Jesus said:

"Everyone who hears these words of mine and does them will be like a wise man who built his house upon the rock; and the rain fell, and the floods came, and the winds blew and beat upon that house, but it did not fall, because it had been founded on rock. And every one who hears these words of mine and does not do them will be like a foolish man who built his house upon the sand; and the rain fell, and the floods came, and the winds blew and beat against that house, and it fell, and great was the fall of it." (Matthew 7:24-27)[1]

Fun is great, but it is not enough. Common interests are fabulous, but they are not enough. Building relationships upon fun or common interests is like building a house on sand. Great relationships need common purpose. Building relationships upon the common purpose of helping each other become the best-version-of-ourselves is like building a house on rock.

If you want to build your relationships on sand, choose your friends based on whether or not they are good-looking, fun, athletic, rich, and popular. If you want to build your relationships on rock, choose friends of good character, who are striving for virtue, who help you become the best-version-of-yourself, and lead you closer to God.

The more closely we align ourselves with the purpose of anything, the more success we will have. Relationships have a purpose. God gives us relationships to help us become the best-version-of-ourselves.

The beautiful thing about the purpose of relationships is that it is unchanging. Like the rock that the wise man built his house on, common purpose is a solid foundation to build your relationships upon. Many things may change in your life over the next month, year, or decade, but the purpose of relationships will not.

Are you ready to start building your relationships on a solid foundation?

DISCUSSION

1. WHO ARE THE MOST IMPORTANT PEOPLE IN YOUR LIFE? WHY?

2. WHAT IS THE PURPOSE OF RELATIONSHIPS?

3. WHAT ARE YOU PRETENDING NOT TO KNOW ABOUT YOUR APPROACH TO RELATIONSHIPS?

144 | DECISION POINT

♥ **RELATIONSHIPS** | 145

STEP 4 — JOURNAL

8 MIN

INSTRUCTIONS: It's time to journal. Remind them that this is a sacred time. Invite your class to open up to page 163 and take a few minutes in silence to journal their answers to those questions.

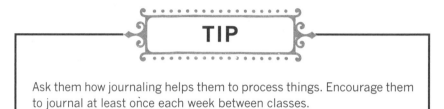

TIP

Ask them how journaling helps them to process things. Encourage them to journal at least once each week between classes.

STEP 5 — ANNOUNCEMENTS

3 MIN

Tip

Thank them for coming. Remind them that you are praying for them, and ask them to pray for you or for someone in your life. Half the challenge is getting these young people out of themselves, getting them to think about someone other than themselves. Inviting them to pray for a sick child you know, or a tough meeting you are going to have next week, or the people of a region of the world affected by a recent natural disaster is a good way to do that.

STEP 6 CLOSING PRAYER

5 MIN

TIP

Begin with the sign of the cross. Then invite the class to lift up to God any of the relationships in their lives that they would like God to bless. Give them thirty to forty seconds to pray in their hearts. Now read the Psalm slowly.

Close with a spontaneous prayer inviting God to help these young people make good relationship decisions.

PSALM 25

To thee, O Lord, I lift up my soul.

2 O my God, in thee I trust, let me not be put to shame; let not my enemies exult over me.

3 Yea, let none that wait for thee be put to shame; let them be ashamed who are wantonly treacherous.

4 Make me to know thy ways, O Lord; teach me thy paths.

5 Lead me in thy truth, and teach me, for thou art the God of my salvation; for thee I wait all the day long.

6 Be mindful of thy mercy, O Lord, and of thy steadfast love, for they have been from of old.

7 Remember not the sins of my youth, or my transgressions; according to thy steadfast love remember me, for thy goodness' sake, O Lord!

8 Good and upright is the Lord; therefore he instructs sinners in the way.

9 He leads the humble in what is right, and teaches the humble his way.

10 All the paths of the Lord are steadfast love and faithfulness, for those who keep his covenant and his testimonies.

11 For thy name's sake, O Lord, pardon my guilt, for it is great.

12 Who is the man that fears the Lord? Him will he instruct in the way that he should choose.

13 He himself shall abide in prosperity, and his children shall possess the land.

14 The friendship of the Lord is for those who fear him, and he makes known to them his covenant.

15 My eyes are ever toward the Lord, for he will pluck my feet out of the net.

16 Turn thou to me, and be gracious to me; for I am lonely and afflicted.

17 Relieve the troubles of my heart, and bring me out of my distresses.

18 Consider my affliction and my trouble, and forgive all my sins.

19 Consider how many are my foes, and with what violent hatred they hate me.

20 Oh guard my life, and deliver me; let me not be put to shame, for I take refuge in thee.

21 May integrity and uprightness preserve me, for I wait for thee.

22 Redeem Israel, O God, out of all his troubles.

The EUCHARIST

My Lord and my God, I firmly believe that you are present in the Eucharist. Take the blindness from my eyes, so that I can see all people and things as you see them. Take the deafness from my ears, so that I can hear your truth and follow it. Take the hardness from my heart, so that I can live and love generously. Give me the grace to receive the Eucharist with humility, so that you can transform me a little more each day into the person you created me to be. Amen.

— *Matthew Kelly* —

QUICK SESSION OVERVIEW

STEP 1	WELCOME
STEP 2	OPENING PRAYER
STEP 3	ENGAGE – WATCH & DISCUSS
STEP 4	JOURNAL
STEP 5	ANNOUNCEMENTS
STEP 6	CLOSING PRAYER

SESSION SEVEN: THE EUCHARIST

Objectives:

- To demonstrate that there are many myths surrounding the Eucharist and to dispel those myths.

- To establish that Jesus is truly present in the Eucharist and that it is an incredible gift to each of us through the Church.

- To teach candidates how to enter into a eucharistic relationship with God, and explain the transformational power the Eucharist can have in their lives.

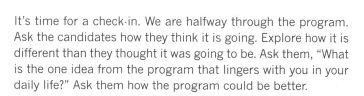

It's time for a check-in. We are halfway through the program. Ask the candidates how they think it is going. Explore how it is different than they thought it was going to be. Ask them, "What is the one idea from the program that lingers with you in your daily life?" Ask them how the program could be better.

 LEADER GUIDE KEY

TIME-ICON: This icon serves as a guide to help you plan approximately how long each activity will take.

[WB5] This code serves as a reference to point you to the page in the Workbook where you can find the related activity/ content.

Example: **[WB5]** *points you to page 5 in the Workbook*

The flag icon is the halfway mark and suggests a good breaking point if your program runs twenty-four classes (or approximately 60 minutes) instead of twelve 120 minute classes.

STEP 2 OPENING PRAYER ························

Tip

Thank them for coming. Tell them you are happy to see them. Invite them to be still and quiet as you begin with a prayer.

Read the prayer slowly and deliberately.

When you have finished, ask them what idea from the prayer struck them the most. The more you can engage them in conversation, the more they will make the content their own. Conversation equals engagement.

3 MIN

My Lord and my God, I firmly believe that you are present in the Eucharist. Take the blindness from my eyes, so that I can see all people and things as you see them. Take the deafness from my ears, so that I can hear your truth and follow it. Take the hardness from my heart, so that I can live and love generously. Give me the grace to receive the Eucharist with humility, so that you can transform me a little more each day into the person you created me to be. Amen.

Matthew Kelly

SESSION 7 INTRODUCTION

WATCH VIDEO

9 MIN

TIP:

Give them a preview. Tell them why they are going to like this short film. Explain what you liked the most. "The thing I really liked about this short film was . . ." But make sure you don't give away too much. This also lets them know that you are preparing for your time together with them.

DISCUSSION QUESTION

6 MIN

1) What is the one idea in this short film that you found most helpful?

SESSION 7.1 **THE ONE THING**

WATCH VIDEO

6 MIN

10 MIN

DISCUSSION QUESTIONS [WB170]

Tip Research shows that Catholics who believe that Jesus is truly present in the Eucharist don't leave the Catholic Church to join other churches. This session could be the difference for some of these young people in whether they remain Catholic their whole lives or not.

1) What is your favorite thing about being Catholic?

2) Which of Jesus' teachings do you find most difficult to live?

3) If you had to spend the rest of your life on a desert island and you could only take five people with you, whom would you take?

Invite a student to read aloud **"Who Was Saint Francis de Sales?"** Ask the student which of their possessions they feel most attached to. [WB173]

TIP!

In many cases the answer will be, "My cell phone." Ask the student, "Do you think you have an unhealthy attachment to your cell phone?" Ask them what they would consider an unhealthy attachment to something. Remember: Keep bringing the conversation back to whether or not things are helping us become-the-best-version-of-ourselves.

AND BY THE HOLY SPIRIT WAS INCARNATE OF THE VIRGIN MARY, AND BECAME MAN. FOR OUR SAKE HE WAS CRUCIFIED UNDER PONTIUS PILATE, HE SUFFERED DEATH AND WAS BURIED, AND ROSE AGAIN ON THE

7.2 the TRUE presence

Grace

GRACE IS THE ASSISTANCE GOD GIVES US TO DO WHAT IS GOOD, TRUE, NOBLE, AND RIGHT.

LUKE 22:19

KNOW IT: Jesus lays down his life for us, giving us his body.

THINK ABOUT IT: We are all called to make sacrifices throughout our lives. Are you willing to make sacrifices that benefit other people? If not, why not?

LIVE IT: How are you being called to lay down your life for others?

You might be thinking to yourself, "I'm not sure if I believe that Jesus is truly present in the host I receive at Mass on Sunday." You wouldn't be the first person to have doubts. Great faith and great doubt often go hand in hand. There was a priest who lived in Lanciano, Italy, around the year 700, who was plagued with doubts about the true presence . . . until one day. After that day he never again doubted that Jesus was truly present in the Eucharist.

What happened on that day? I'm glad you asked.

On that day, the priest was celebrating Mass in the small church, even though he was filled with doubts about the real presence of Jesus in the Eucharist. As he said the Words of Consecration ("Take this, all of you, and eat of it, for this is my body which will be given up for you.") the bread changed into living flesh and the wine changed into blood, before his eyes.

Today, you can go to Lanciano and see the flesh and blood that has remained there for more than thirteen hundred years. The flesh and blood have been studied by scientists on a number of occasions, and the following conclusions have been drawn: The flesh is real human flesh and the blood is real human blood, the flesh is muscular tissue from the heart, and there is no evidence of preservatives or any other chemical agents present.

This is one of thousands of Eucharistic miracles that have been documented throughout the life of the Church.

At the Last Supper Jesus "took the bread, and when he had given thanks, he broke it and gave it to them, saying, 'This is my body, which is given for you. Do this in remembrance of me,'" (Luke 22:19) We take Jesus at his word. At Mass on Sunday the priest extends his hands over simple bread and wine and asks the Holy Spirit to transform them into the body and blood of Jesus Christ.

If the Holy Spirit can do that to bread and wine, imagine what he can do with you if you open yourself up to the experience of Confirmation.

You are not just a body. You are a delicate composition of body and soul. If you haven't already, one day you will discover you need to feed your soul in order to live a full and happy life. And when that day comes I want you to remember today, because there is no better way to feed your soul than with the Eucharist.

The Eucharist is astonishing. God himself wants to nourish us. God himself wants to feed us spiritually. God wants to dwell in you.

Some people say that the bread and wine are just a symbol of Jesus' body and blood, but that is not what we believe as Catholics. And the evidence found in Divine Revelation suggests that it is not just a symbol. The Scriptures don't suggest the symbol. Jesus didn't say, "Unless you eat a symbol of my flesh and drink a symbol of my blood you will not have life." And remember there are two aspects of Divine Revelation: Scripture and Tradition. And from the earliest times, Christians have believed that the Eucharist was the body and blood of the Risen Jesus, and not just a symbol.

Can I prove it to you scientifically? No. Not everything can be explained or proven scientifically. If you could prove everything scientifically, there would be no need for faith. There is such a thing as mystery. We human beings don't know everything. If we did we would be God, and there is plenty of evidence in our daily lives that confirms that human beings are not God. Life is full of mystery, and mystery is a beautiful thing.

At the heart of the mystery that is the Catholic faith is the Eucharist. I hope with every passing year of your life you will explore and embrace the mystery of the Eucharist more.

The wiser you become, the closer you will want to be to God. And God wants to be close to us. Saint Francis de Sales wrote, "In the Eucharist we become one with God." To be one with God is a beautiful thing, and whether you are aware of it or not, it is your deepest yearning. You have an insatiable yearning to be one with God. I hope you will start listening to that yearning.

If you want to have a life-changing experience, find an Adoration Chapel in your area and visit it. Sit there in Jesus' presence for one hour. You will be amazed how powerful Jesus' presence is, and how much he will teach you about yourself and your life in one hour.

Who Was St. FRANCIS de SALES?

Saint Francis de Sales (1567-1622) was a priest and bishop and is regarded as one of the great spiritual writers of all time. During his era it was widely believed that holiness was only for monks and nuns, but he banished that idea. The central theme in his classic *Introduction to the Devout Life* is the idea that God calls every man and woman to live a holy life. Francis also spoke about the allure of money and things, pointing out that the danger of possessions is how easily they can possess us. Possessions increase our happiness only when we use them for our good and the good of others. Francis de Sales is the patron saint of writers and his feast day is January 24.

All the **ANSWERS** *are in the* **TABERNACLE.**

SESSION 7.2 **THE TRUE PRESENCE**

6 MIN

WATCH VIDEO

 TIP

Tell them they are about to hear an incredible story that will change the way they experience Mass forever.

10 MIN

DISCUSSION QUESTIONS [WB174]

1) Is there a person in your life whose presence just makes you feel calm and safe?

2) When did you first learn about Jesus being present in the Eucharist?

3) How do you think your life would change if you spent one hour each week sitting quietly in Jesus' presence?

SESSION 7.3 THE POWER OF THE EUCHARIST

WATCH VIDEO

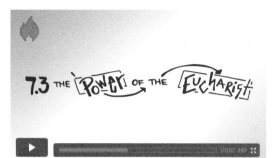

3 MIN

Listening skills are essential in order to live a rich and rewarding life. It is impossible to have great relationships unless you are a good listener. But most people are not good listeners. Explain to the candidates that one of the practical life skills they are developing throughout this program is the ability to really listen. Encourage them to listen to each other with respect.

DISCUSSION QUESTIONS [WB177]

10 MIN

1) When was the last time you did something that you knew wasn't good for you? Why did you do it if you knew it wasn't good for you?

2) Have you ever tried to quit a bad habit and failed?

3) When you're in a situation and you want to do what is good and right but are attracted to the wrong choice, do you call on God and ask for his help?

EXERCISE: CROSSWORD PUZZLE

5 MIN

Tip

Ask each candidate to calculate how many Sundays they have left if they live until they are eighty-five. Talk to them about how that makes them feel. Tell them how many you have left, and how fast they pass.

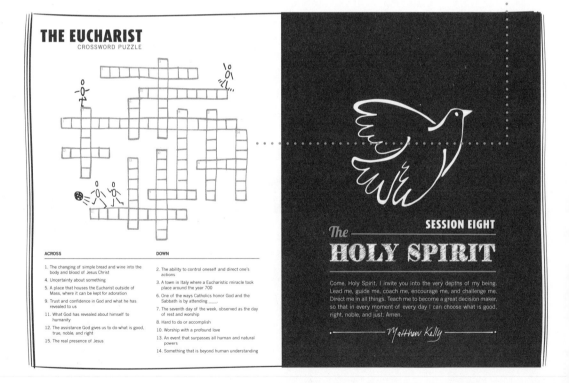

THE EUCHARIST
CROSSWORD PUZZLE

ACROSS

1. The changing of simple bread and wine into the body and blood of Jesus Christ

4. Uncertainty about something

5. A place that houses the Eucharist outside of Mass, where it can be kept for adoration

9. Trust and confidence in God and what he has revealed to us

11. What God has revealed about himself to humanity

12. The assistance God gives us to do what is good, true, noble, and right

15. The real presence of Jesus

DOWN

2. The ability to control oneself and direct one's actions

3. A town in Italy where a Eucharistic miracle took place around the year 700

6. One of the ways Catholics honor God and the Sabbath is by attending ____.

7. The seventh day of the week, observed as the day of rest and worship

8. Hard to do or accomplish

10. Worship with a profound love

13. An event that surpasses all human and natural powers

14. Something that is beyond human understanding

SESSION EIGHT

The HOLY SPIRIT

Come, Holy Spirit, I invite you into the very depths of my being. Lead me, guide me, coach me, encourage me, and challenge me. Direct me in all things. Teach me to become a great decision maker, so that in every moment of every day I can choose what is good, right, noble, and just. Amen.

— *Matthew Kelly* —

SESSION 7.4 GET CLOSE AND STAY CLOSE

WATCH VIDEO

Before you start this short film, ask the candidates to bring to mind the most beautiful church they have ever been in.

5 MIN

DISCUSSION QUESTIONS [WB182]

10 MIN

1) If you could visit one of the beautiful churches mentioned in this section, which would you choose?

2) At this time in your life, what question would you like Jesus to answer for you? (Your question should be about something that applies directly to you).

3) What quiet places have you found to spend a few minutes in each day?

EXERCISE VIRTUE IN FOCUS

TIP

🕐 **5 MIN**

This session highlights the virtue of temperance. Invite a candidate to read aloud the **Virtue in Focus** section. Choose one of the questions from the section and invite the candidates to share their answers. [WB184]

BELIEVE IN THE HOLY SPIRIT, THE LORD, THE GIVER OF LIFE, WHO PROCEEDS FROM THE FATHER AND THE

7.5 DECISION point

VIRTUE IN FOCUS

Tem·per·ance
[tem-per-uh ns]

Controlling your thoughts, words, actions, and feelings.

Who do you know who exemplifies this virtue?

In what area of your life do you find it most difficult to practice temperance?

What is one way you can become more temperate this week?

What do you think Mary had planned for her life before the angel appeared to her?

Every Sunday morning you make a decision. It's the biggest decision of your week. To go or not to go, that is the question.

You might say that Mass is boring. I was bored at Mass for a long time, but then something happened. I started listening to what God was trying to say to me. I got myself a little journal and took it to Mass with me, and each week I wrote down the one thing that I felt God was saying to me. I have been doing this for fifteen years now. Each year I get a new journal. At home in my study, where I write, I have these fifteen journals on a shelf. When I get writer's block I pick one up and just start reading. Some days when I don't feel like praying I take one of these journals and just talk to God about some of the things he has said to me over the years. It is amazing the things God will say to us when we start listening.

I hope you go to Mass every Sunday for the rest of your lives so that God can nourish you with the Eucharist, but I also hope you will start to appreciate the bigger picture.

God has declared Sunday—the Sabbath day—as a day of rest. In Genesis 2:2 we read about God resting on the seventh day. Why? Why did God rest? Was he tired? No. God is a pure spirit and as such does not experience fatigue like we human beings do. So, why did he rest? He rested because he foresaw our need for rest. He wanted to show us how to live. He wanted to demonstrate that rest is a good thing, and something that we all need.

You have a legitimate need for rest. The Sabbath is God's response to your physical and spiritual need for rest and renewal. And nothing will renew you like receiving the Eucharist. It is literally food from Heaven.

On average you will live for another seventy years. That means you have 3,640 Sundays left. Don't waste a single one. It may seem like a lot, but you will be amazed at how quickly life passes. It feels like six months ago I was sitting where you are preparing for Confirmation . . . but that was twenty-five years ago.

You have a lot of decisions to make. Getting yourself to Mass on Sunday and receiving the Eucharist will help you make better decisions in every area of your life.

JOURNAL QUESTIO

1. WHY DO YOU THINK OUR CULTURE HAS REJECTED THE SABBATH?

2. HOW CAN YOU HONOR THE SABBATH AS A DAY OF REST?

3. HOW WOULD THE WORLD BE DIFFERENT IF EVERYONE TOOK ONE D AND TURN THEIR ATTENTION TOWARD GOD?

WATCH VIDEO

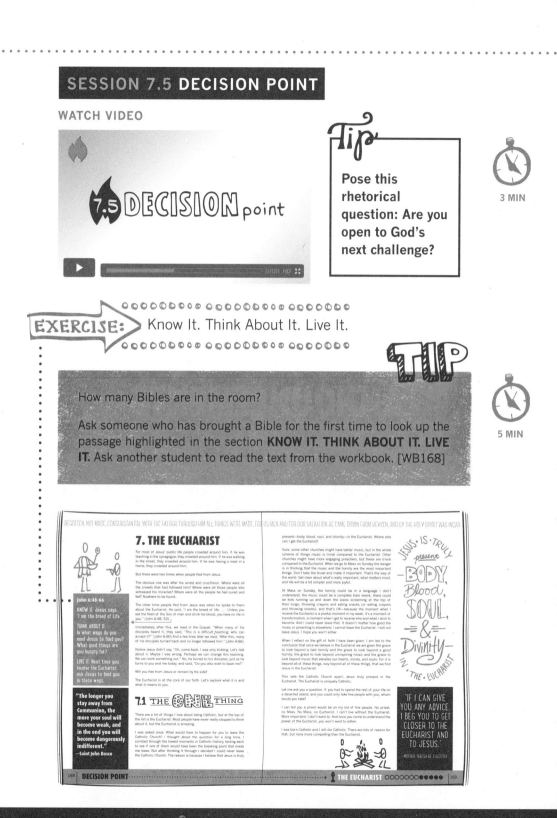

7.5 DECISION point

Tip

Pose this rhetorical question: Are you open to God's next challenge?

3 MIN

EXERCISE: Know It. Think About It. Live It.

TIP

How many Bibles are in the room?

Ask someone who has brought a Bible for the first time to look up the passage highlighted in the section **KNOW IT. THINK ABOUT IT. LIVE IT.** Ask another student to read the text from the workbook. [WB168]

5 MIN

BEGOTTEN, NOT MADE, CONSUBSTANTIAL WITH THE FATHER; THROUGH HIM ALL THINGS WERE MADE. FOR US MEN AND FOR OUR SALVATION HE CAME DOWN FROM HEAVEN, AND BY THE HOLY SPIRIT WAS INCAR-

7. THE EUCHARIST

For most of Jesus' public life people crowded around him. If he was teaching in the synagogue, they crowded around him. If he was walking in the street, they crowded around him. If he was having a meal in a home, they crowded around him.

But there were two times when people fled from Jesus.

The obvious one was after his arrest and crucifixion. Where were all the crowds that had followed him? Where were all those people who witnessed his miracles? Where were all the people he had cured and fed? Nowhere to be found.

The other time people fled from Jesus was when he spoke to them about the Eucharist. He said, "I am the bread of life . . . Unless you eat the flesh of the Son of man and drink his blood, you have no life in you." (John 6:48, 53)

Immediately after this, we read in the Gospel: "When many of his disciples heard it, they said, 'This is a difficult teaching; who can accept it?'" (John 6:60) And a few lines later we read, "After this, many of his disciples turned back and no longer followed him." (John 6:66)

Notice Jesus didn't say, "Oh, come back. I was only kidding. Let's talk about it. Maybe I was wrong. Perhaps we can change this teaching. We can work something out." No, he turned to his disciples, just as he turns to you and me today, and said, "Do you also wish to leave me?"

Will you flee from Jesus or remain by his side?

The Eucharist is at the core of our faith. Let's explore what it is and what it means to you.

7.1 THE ONE THING

There are a lot of things I love about being Catholic, but at the top of the list is the Eucharist. Most people have never really stopped to think about it, but the Eucharist is amazing.

I was asked once: What would have to happen for you to leave the Catholic Church? I thought about the question for a long time. I combed through the lowest moments in Catholic history, testing each to see if one of them would have been the breaking point that made me leave. But after thinking it through I decided I could never leave the Catholic Church. The reason is because I believe that Jesus is truly

present—body, blood, soul, and divinity—in the Eucharist. Where else can I get the Eucharist?

Sure, some other churches might have better music, but in the whole scheme of things music is trivial compared to the Eucharist. Other churches might have more engaging preachers, but these are trivial compared to the Eucharist. When we go to Mass on Sunday the danger is in thinking that the music and the homily are the most important things. Don't take the trivial and make it important. That's the way of the world. Get clear about what's really important, what matters most, and life will be a lot simpler and more joyful.

At Mass on Sunday, the homily could be in a language I don't understand, the music could be a complete train wreck, there could be kids running up and down the aisles screaming at the top of their lungs, throwing crayons and eating snacks (or eating snacks and throwing snacks), and that's OK—because the moment when I receive the Eucharist is a pivotal moment in my week. It's a moment of transformation, a moment when I get to receive who and what I wish to become. And I could never leave that. It doesn't matter how good the music or preaching is elsewhere; I cannot leave the Eucharist. I will not leave Jesus. I hope you won't either.

When I reflect on the gift of faith I have been given, I am led to the conclusion that once we believe in the Eucharist we are given the grace to look beyond a bad homily and the grace to look beyond a good homily; the grace to look beyond uninspiring music and the grace to look beyond music that elevates our hearts, minds, and souls. For it is beyond all of these things, way beyond all of these things, that we find Jesus in the Eucharist.

This sets the Catholic Church apart: Jesus truly present in the Eucharist. The Eucharist is uniquely Catholic.

Let me ask you a question. If you had to spend the rest of your life on a deserted island, and you could only take five people with you, whom would you take?

I can tell you a priest would be on my list of five people. No priest, no Mass. No Mass, no Eucharist. I can't live without the Eucharist. More important, I don't want to. And once you come to understand the power of the Eucharist, you won't want to either.

I was born Catholic and will die Catholic. There are lots of reason for that, but none more compelling than the Eucharist.

John 6:48-66

KNOW IT: Jesus says, "I am the bread of life."

THINK ABOUT IT: In what ways do you need Jesus to feed you? What good things are you hungry for?

LIVE IT: Next time you receive the Eucharist ask Jesus to feed you in these ways.

"The longer you stay away from Communion, the more your soul will become weak, and in the end you will become dangerously indifferent."
—Saint John Bosco

JESUS IS TRULY present BODY, Blood, SOUL & Divinity— IN THE EUCHARIST

"IF I CAN GIVE YOU ANY ADVICE, I BEG YOU TO GET CLOSER TO THE EUCHARIST AND TO JESUS."
—MOTHER TERESA OF CALCUTTA

168 **DECISION POINT**

THE EUCHARIST 169

STEP 4 JOURNAL

INSTRUCTIONS: It's time to journal. Remind them that this is a sacred time. Invite your class to open up to page 185 and take a few minutes in silence to journal their answers to those questions.

10 MIN

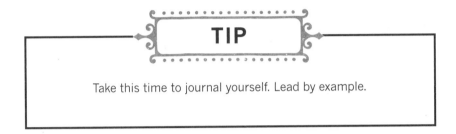

TIP

Take this time to journal yourself. Lead by example.

STEP 5 ANNOUNCEMENTS

3 MIN

Tip

With renewed enthusiasm, thank them for coming. Tell them how much you are getting out of this time with them. Remind them that you are praying for them, and ask them to pray for you.

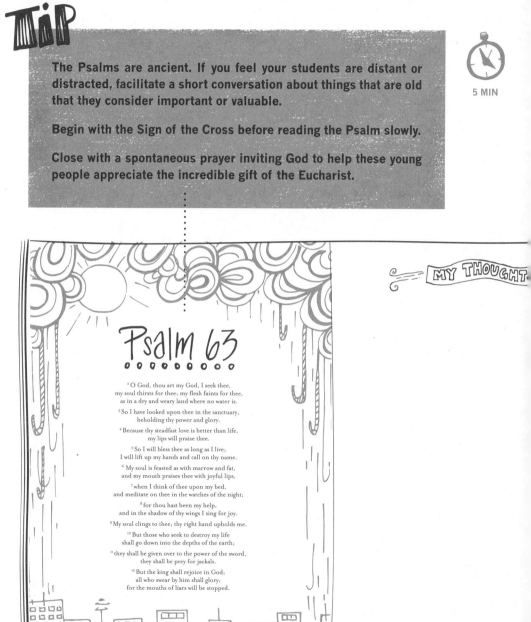

TIP

The Psalms are ancient. If you feel your students are distant or distracted, facilitate a short conversation about things that are old that they consider important or valuable.

Begin with the Sign of the Cross before reading the Psalm slowly.

Close with a spontaneous prayer inviting God to help these young people appreciate the incredible gift of the Eucharist.

5 MIN

MY THOUGHT

Psalm 63

² O God, thou art my God, I seek thee,
my soul thirsts for thee; my flesh faints for thee,
as in a dry and weary land where no water is.

³ So I have looked upon thee in the sanctuary,
beholding thy power and glory.

⁴ Because thy steadfast love is better than life,
my lips will praise thee.

⁵ So I will bless thee as long as I live;
I will lift up my hands and call on thy name.

⁶ My soul is feasted as with marrow and fat,
and my mouth praises thee with joyful lips,

⁷ when I think of thee upon my bed,
and meditate on thee in the watches of the night;

⁸ for thou hast been my help,
and in the shadow of thy wings I sing for joy.

⁹ My soul clings to thee; thy right hand upholds me.

¹⁰ But those who seek to destroy my life
shall go down into the depths of the earth;

¹¹ they shall be given over to the power of the sword,
they shall be prey for jackals.

¹² But the king shall rejoice in God;
all who swear by him shall glory;
for the mouths of liars will be stopped.

THE EUCHARIST

The HOLY SPIRIT

Come, Holy Spirit, I invite you into the very depths of my being. Lead me, guide me, coach me, encourage me, and challenge me. Direct me in all things. Teach me to become a great decision maker, so that in every moment of every day I can choose what is good, right, noble, and just. Amen.

Matthew Kelly

QUICK SESSION OVERVIEW

STEP 1 WELCOME

STEP 2 OPENING PRAYER

STEP 3 ENGAGE – WATCH & DISCUSS

STEP 4 JOURNAL

STEP 5 ANNOUNCEMENTS

STEP 6 CLOSING PRAYER

SESSION EIGHT: THE HOLY SPIRIT

Objectives:

- To demonstrate the practical power of the gifts and fruits of the Holy Spirit.

- To help candidates to recognize the promptings of the Holy Spirit.

- To teach candidates to allow the Holy Spirit to guide them in their decisions.

STEP 1 WELCOME

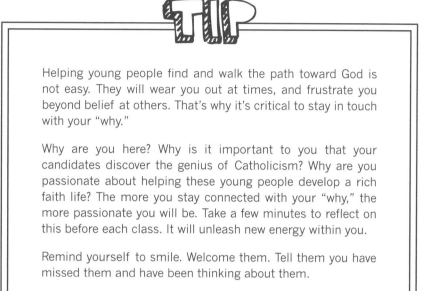

TIP

Helping young people find and walk the path toward God is not easy. They will wear you out at times, and frustrate you beyond belief at others. That's why it's critical to stay in touch with your "why."

Why are you here? Why is it important to you that your candidates discover the genius of Catholicism? Why are you passionate about helping these young people develop a rich faith life? The more you stay connected with your "why," the more passionate you will be. Take a few minutes to reflect on this before each class. It will unleash new energy within you.

Remind yourself to smile. Welcome them. Tell them you have missed them and have been thinking about them.

LEADER GUIDE KEY

TIME-ICON: This icon serves as a guide to help you plan approximately how long each activity will take.

[WB5] This code serves as a reference to point you to the page in the Workbook where you can find the related activity/content.

Example: **[WB5]** *points you to page 5 in the Workbook*

The flag icon is the halfway mark and suggests a good breaking point if your program runs twenty-four classes (or approximately 60 minutes) instead of twelve 120 minute classes.

Tip

Talk about how you love praying with them. Sure, we can pray alone—and we should make time for that every day. But there is something beautiful about praying with other people.

Talk about some of the ways you pray with other people: grace before meals, evening prayers with your children, Sunday Mass, etc. Many of them may not come from families in which they pray before meals. Some of them may come from families that never pray together at all.

Now, begin with the Sign of the Cross and read the prayer slowly and deliberately.

3 MIN

Come, Holy Spirit, I invite you into the very depths of my being. Lead me, guide me, coach me, encourage me, and challenge me. Direct me in all things. Teach me to become a great decision maker, so that in every moment of every day I can choose what is good, right, noble, and just. Amen.

— *Matthew Kelly* —

STEP 3 ENGAGE: WATCH & DISCUSS

SESSION 8 INTRODUCTION

WATCH VIDEO

8 MIN

TIP: There is one phrase that gets repeated over and over in this short film ("Just do the next right thing"). Try to use it throughout this session in your discussions with the candidates. Continue to use it throughout the rest of the program.

DISCUSSION QUESTION

6 MIN

1) What is the one idea in this short film that you found most helpful?

SESSION 8.1 WHO IS THE HOLY SPIRIT?

WATCH VIDEO

9 MIN

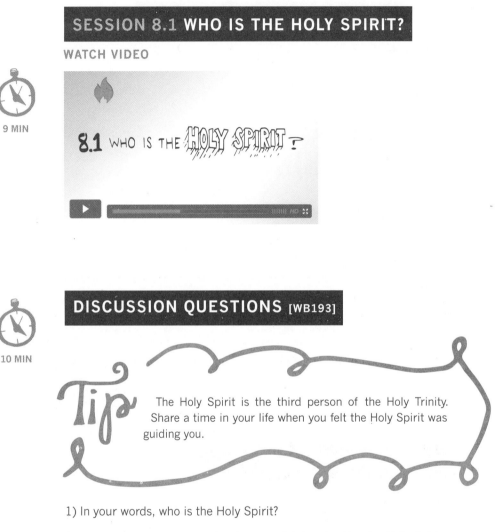

8.1 WHO IS THE HOLY SPIRIT?

DISCUSSION QUESTIONS [WB193]

10 MIN

Tip

The Holy Spirit is the third person of the Holy Trinity. Share a time in your life when you felt the Holy Spirit was guiding you.

1) In your words, who is the Holy Spirit?

2) Describe a time in your life when you felt inspired by the Holy Spirit.

3) Would you like to learn how to experience joy even in the midst of great suffering like Saint Paul? What do you think his secret was?

EXERCISE

Invite a student to read aloud **"Who Was King Solomon?"** Ask the candidates, "If God appeared to you and offered to grant any request, what would your request be?" [WB196]

🕕 6 MIN

TIP! Life is always asking us what we want. We may not hear the question or be aware of it, but life is always asking the question, and we are always answering it. What do you want from life? Explore this with the candidates.

I BELIEVE IN ONE, HOLY, CATHOLIC AND APOSTOLIC CHURCH. I CONFESS ONE BAPTISM FOR THE FORGIVENESS OF SINS AND I LOOK FORWARD TO THE RESURRECTION OF THE DEAD AND THE LIFE OF THE WORLD TO

Matthew 6:33

KNOW IT: Seek first the things of God.

THINK ABOUT IT: What are your priorities? Are they worldly priorities or godly priorities?

LIVE IT: Make God's priorities your own today.

King Solomon?

Solomon was the son of David and King of Israel from c. 970 to 931 BC. The Bible credits Solomon with building the first temple in Jerusalem and portrays him as the wisest man of his time. This wisdom was a gift from God; the first book of Kings recounts how Solomon prayed for wisdom. During his reign he became incredibly wealthy and powerful, but ultimately his sins, which included turning away from God and idolatry, led to the kingdom being torn in two. The story of Solomon teaches us how seductive and disorienting power, fame, and money can be.

8.2 UNOPENED GIFTS

If God appeared to you in a vision and said, "Ask me for anything and I will give it to you," what would you ask him for? Think about it for a moment. Would you ask for money, a long life, success in a career, victory for your favorite sports team?

This is exactly what happened to Solomon, the son of King David. Biblical scholars believe that Solomon was probably only around twelve years old when he became king. In 1 Kings 3:5-15 we read about God appearing to Solomon in a dream and asking what he would like God to give him. Solomon asked for wisdom. In particular, he wanted the wisdom to discern right from wrong, good from evil. This pleased God so much that he granted Solomon wisdom in abundance, but he also granted him riches, honor, and a long life.

Here we find a connection between how God treated Solomon and Jesus' teachings. In Matthew 6:33 we read, "Seek first the kingdom of God and his righteousness, and all these other things will be given to you in addition." This is what Solomon did, and God responded lavishly.

God is a giver of gifts.

One Christmas when I was a child, I half-unwrapped gifts to see what they were, and if the gift was not the one thing I was looking for, I wouldn't even finish unwrapping it; I would just move on to the next parcel. I remember opening one of those half-unwrapped gifts a few days later and realizing that I had misjudged the importance and value of the gift.

At Baptism you received the seven gifts of the Holy Spirit, but you may not have fully unwrapped them yet. At Confirmation these gifts will be strengthened in you; the question is, how will you respond to them?

I could put a million dollars in a bank account for you, but if you ignored it and never used it, it wouldn't do you any good. The gifts of the Holy Spirit are worth more than many millions of dollars, but if you don't engage them and nurture them, you will not experience all that they have to offer.

How was Mary different from Solomon?

So, what are the seven gifts of the Holy Spirit?

1. Wisdom: The ability to discern what is true, right, and lasting. Wisdom enables us to see life from God's perspective. It helps you to establish the right priorities in your life, and leads you to think and act in mature ways.

2. Understanding: Allows you to look beyond the shallowness of the world and see the lasting truth in every situation, by recognizing how God is working in our lives.

3. Counsel: The right judgment that allows us to see what is right and what is wrong, and the prudence to act accordingly.

4. Fortitude: The courage and strength of will to do what you know you should, even if that means personal loss or suffering.

5. Knowledge: The ability to see things from a supernatural viewpoint. In particular, to know what God is asking of you.

6. Piety: A loyalty to God that manifests as generous love and affectionate obedience. This is the gift that allows you to love and worship God as he deserves to be loved and worshipped.

7. Fear of the Lord (Reverence): Helps us to grasp God's greatness and our dependence on him. As a result, we are filled with enormous respect for God and we dread above all offending him or being separated from him. Our Jewish ancestors believed that fear of the Lord was the beginning of wisdom. Of course, it is not a fear like we usually think of today. It is more like an overwhelming sense of not wanting to disappoint the One who has done (and continues to do) so much for us.

These are the seven gifts of the Holy Spirit. When the bishop prays over you at your Confirmation, he will be praying that you are filled with them. Each of these gifts helps you to become the-best-version-of-yourself and live the life God created you to live.

Every day you face situations that require these gifts. We have taken a few minutes to explore them, but I want to encourage you to delve into them more. If you don't know what they are, you won't use them. Knowing them is essential if you are going to activate them in your daily life.

GET THE APP!

WHAT YOU CHOOSE TO THINK ABOUT IS A REALLY IMPORTANT CHOICE YOU MAKE EVERY DAY.

· GIFTS ·
OF · THE · SPIRIT

WISDOM
Understanding
COUNSEL
FORTITUDE
KNOWLEDGE
Piety
FEAR OF THE LORD (REVERENCE

6 MIN

SESSION 8.2 **UNOPENED GIFTS**

WATCH VIDEO

8.2 UNOPENED GIFTS

10 MIN

TIP

Before you start the short film, ask them about the gifts of the Holy Spirit. How many are there? What are they? See how much your students already know.

DISCUSSION QUESTIONS [WB198]

1) Have you ever given someone a gift and felt he or she was ungrateful? How did that make you feel?

2) Which of the seven gifts of the Holy Spirit do you feel most in need of at this time in your life?

3) How would your life be better if you really opened yourself up to the gifts of the Holy Spirit?

SESSION 8.3 THE FRUITS OF THE HOLY SPIRIT

WATCH VIDEO

5 MIN

TIP

Be you. Throughout your time together with these young people, make sure they are getting to know you. If you like sports trivia, use that as an icebreaker. If you love chocolate, give it for prizes. If you love music, play some of your favorite songs for them as they come into class each time. Let them get to know you.

DISCUSSION QUESTIONS [WB202]

10 MIN

1) Which person in your life would you like to fill with joy?

2) How would a lack of self-control make it harder to experience the eleven fruits of the Holy Spirit?

3) Can you see how God's ways are designed to bring order to our lives and liberate us from worldly chaos?

EXERCISE:

6 MIN

Tip

Ask a candidate to read aloud the quote from Saint Ignatius of Loyola on page 194. Invite the class to talk about the idea that struck them the most.

THE GOAL OF OUR LIFE IS TO LIVE WITH GOD FOREVER.
God, who loves us, gave us life.
OUR OWN RESPONSE OF LOVE ALLOWS GOD'S LIFE
to flow into us WITHOUT LIMIT.

All the things in this world are **GIFTS FROM GOD**,
Presented to us so that WE CAN KNOW GOD MORE EASILY
AND MAKE *a return of love* MORE READILY.
As a result, we appreciate and use all these gifts of God
Insofar as they help us TO DEVELOP AS LOVING PERSONS.
But if any of these gifts become the *center of our lives*,
THEY DISPLACE GOD
And so hinder our growth toward our goal.

In everyday life, then, we must hold ourselves in balance
Before all of these created gifts
insofar as **WE HAVE A CHOICE**
And are not bound by some obligation.
WE SHOULD NOT FIX OUR DESIRES on health or sickness,
Wealth or poverty, success or failure, a long life or a short one.
For everything has the potential of *calling forth* in us
A DEEPER RESPONSE TO OUR LIFE IN GOD.

Our only desire and our **ONE CHOICE** should be this:
I WANT AND I CHOOSE WHAT BETTER LEADS
TO GOD'S *deepening* HIS LIFE IN ME.

St. Ignatius of Loyola

🕊 **THE HOLY SPIRIT** ○○○○

SESSION 8.4 PROMPTED

WATCH VIDEO

Ask them if they have been practicing the Prayer Process. If not, why not?

7 MIN

DISCUSSION QUESTIONS [WB207]

10 MIN

1) If you were going to go on a pilgrimage and walk the Camino, whom would you take with you?

2) When was the last time you felt the Holy Spirit prompting you to do something?

3) What is your favorite part of The Prayer Process? Why?

195

EXERCISE — VIRTUE IN FOCUS

TIP

6 MIN

This session highlights the virtue of gentleness. Invite a candidate to read aloud the **Virtue in Focus** section. Choose one of the questions from the section and encourage the candidates to share their answers. [WB201]

RESURRECTION OF THE DEAD AND THE LIFE OF THE WORLD TO COME. AMEN. I BELIEVE IN ONE GOD, THE FATHER ALMIGHTY, MAKER OF HEAVEN AND EARTH, OF ALL THINGS VISIBLE AND IN

8.3 The Fruits of the Holy Spirit

How do we know if we are filled with the Holy Spirit? How will you know if you are seeking God's loving plan for your life and responding to it? Jesus advises us that we can judge a tree by its fruits. "A good tree cannot bear bad fruit, nor can a bad tree bear good fruit." (Matthew 7:18) What fruit is your life bearing today? What fruit do you want your life to bear in the future? What fruit do you think God wants you to bear?

If we are really allowing the Holy Spirit to flourish within us, the fruits should be bubbling forth in our lives. Those fruits are: love, joy, peace, patience, kindness, goodness, generosity, gentleness, faithfulness, modesty, self-control, and chastity.

You might not know it yet, but these are the things you want. You want these fruits more than anything else you have ever wanted. In fact, every yearning you have is for these things. We try to substitute other things for them, but it never works.

Embracing and engaging the gifts of the Holy Spirit that we spoke about earlier—wisdom, understanding, counsel, fortitude, knowledge, piety, and fear of the Lord—is the path that leads to the fruit of the Holy Spirit.

Let's take a look at the twelve fruits of the Holy Spirit.

Love: To love God above all things and to love others as God calls us to.

Joy: This is more than just being happy. It is a feeling awakened by the possession or expectation of something good. And this joy can be present deep within us even when things don't go our way.

Peace: The serenity and tranquility that flows from order. The world can make our lives disordered and chaotic. God wants to bring order to our lives – and with that order comes a deep and abiding peace.

Patience: Enables us to endure inconvenience, difficulties, and hardship without complaint.

Kindness: Concern for others who are in trouble or in need.

Goodness: Doing what is good and right in every circumstance.

Generosity: To give freely of our time, talent, and treasure beyond what justice requires.

Gentleness: To be submissive to God and considerate of others.

Faithfulness: To be reliable and trustworthy.

Modesty: The moderation of our speech, dress, and behavior.

Self-control: The control of our desires so that we can focus them on what is good and right.

Chastity: The moderation of desire for sexual pleasure according to right reason, faith, and state in life.

If you really take the time to consider what you want from life, you will discover that a life filled with the fruit of the Holy Spirit is what you are yearning for. If you consider the opposite of each of the fruits, you will discover that they lead to a life of slavery and misery.

When we reject the fruit of the Holy Spirit we fall into a life of sin. Sin rejects God's design for who we are and the way we should live our lives. In doing so, sin rejects order and embraces the chaos of disorder. This disorder robs us of the tranquility and peace that God desires for us. When your room is tidy and things are in the places they belong, there is a certain peace and tranquility that comes from that. If your room is a mess, with things scattered all around, the chaos of that environment robs you of peace and tranquility and creates anxiousness.

The way of God is one of peace and order. The way of sin is one of chaos and anxiousness. Which will you choose?

VIRTUE IN FOCUS

Gen·tle·ness
[jen-tl-ness]

mildness of speech, temperament, and behavior; kindness and tenderness

Who do you know who exemplifies the virtue of gentleness?

In what ways is God calling you to be gentle with others?

How is God inviting you to be gentle with yourself?

"DO NOT BE AFRAID.
DO NOT BE SATISFIED
WITH MEDIOCRITY.
PUT OUT INTO THE DEEP
AND LET DOWN YOUR
NETS FOR A CATCH."

—JOHN PAUL II

POINT ➤ **THE HOLY SPIRIT** ○○○○○○○○●●●● | 201

WATCH VIDEO

Ask them what they think the challenge will be.

3 MIN

EXERCISE: Know It. Think About It. Live It.

6 MIN

Invite everyone with a Bible to open to one of your favorite passages. Tell them why it is one of your favorites.

Ask someone to read aloud the Bible passage highlighted in the section **KNOW IT. THINK ABOUT IT. LIVE IT.** Ask another student to read the text from the workbook. [WB196]

BELIEVE IN ONE, HOLY, CATHOLIC AND APOSTOLIC CHURCH. I CONFESS ONE BAPTISM FOR THE FORGIVENESS OF SINS AND I LOOK FORWARD TO THE RESURRECTION OF THE DEAD AND THE LIFE OF THE WORLD TO

Matthew 6:33

KNOW IT: Seek first the things of God.

THINK ABOUT IT: What are your priorities? Are they worldly priorities or godly priorities?

LIVE IT: Make God's priorities your own today.

KING Solomon?

Solomon was the son of David and King of Israel from c. 970 to 931 BC. The Bible credits Solomon with building the first temple in Jerusalem and portrays him as the wisest man of his time. This wisdom was a gift from God: the first book of Kings recounts how Solomon prayed for wisdom. During his reign he became incredibly wealthy and powerful, but ultimately his sins, which included turning away from God and idolatry, led to the kingdom being torn in two. The story of Solomon teaches us how seductive and disorienting power, fame, and money can be.

8.2 UNOPENED GIFTS

If God appeared to you in a vision and said, "Ask me for anything and I will give it to you," what would you ask him for? Think about it for a moment. Would you ask for money, a long life, success in a career, victory for your favorite sports team?

This is exactly what happened to Solomon, the son of King David. Biblical scholars believe that Solomon was probably only around twelve years old when he became king. In 1 Kings 3:5-15 we read about God appearing to Solomon in a dream and asking what he would like God to give him. Solomon asked for wisdom. In particular, he wanted the wisdom to discern right from wrong, good from evil. This pleased God so much that he granted Solomon wisdom in abundance, but he also granted him riches, honor, and a long life.

Here we find a connection between how God treated Solomon and Jesus' teachings. In Matthew 6:33 we read, "Seek first the kingdom of God and his righteousness, and all these other things will be given to you in addition." This is what Solomon did, and God responded lavishly.

God is a giver of gifts.

One Christmas when I was a child, I half-unwrapped gifts to see what they were, and if the gift was not the one thing I was looking for. I wouldn't even finish unwrapping it; I would just move on to the next parcel. I remember opening one of those half-unwrapped gifts a few days later and realizing that I had misjudged the importance and value of the gift.

At Baptism you received the seven gifts of the Holy Spirit, but you may not have fully unwrapped them yet. At Confirmation these gifts will be strengthened in you; the question is, how will you respond to them?

I could put a million dollars in a bank account for you, but if you ignored it and never used it, it wouldn't do you any good. The gifts of the Holy Spirit are worth more than many millions of dollars, but if you don't engage them and nurture them, you will not experience all that they have to offer.

How was Mary different from Solomon?

So, what are the seven gifts of the Holy Spirit?

1. Wisdom: The ability to discern what is true, right, and lasting. Wisdom enables us to see life from God's perspective. It helps you to establish the right priorities in your life, and leads you to think and act in mature ways.

2. Understanding: Allows you to look beyond the shallowness of the world and see the lasting truth in every situation, by recognizing how God is working in our lives.

3. Counsel: The right judgment that allows us to see what is right and what is wrong, and the prudence to act accordingly.

4. Fortitude: The courage and strength of will to do what you know you should, even if that means personal loss or suffering.

5. Knowledge: The ability to see things from a supernatural viewpoint. In particular, to know what God is asking of you.

6. Piety: A loyalty to God that manifests as generous love and affectionate obedience. This is the gift that allows you to love and worship God as he deserves to be loved and worshipped.

7. Fear of the Lord (Reverence): Helps us to grasp God's greatness and our dependence on him. As a result, we are filled with enormous respect for God and we dread above all offending him or being separated from him. Our Jewish ancestors believed that fear of the Lord was the beginning of wisdom. Of course, it is not a fear like we usually think of fear today. It is more like an overwhelming sense of not wanting to disappoint the One who has done (and continues to do) so much for us.

These are the seven gifts of the Holy Spirit. When the bishop prays over you at your Confirmation, he will be praying that you are filled with them. Each of these gifts helps you to become the best version of-yourself and live the life God created you to live.

Every day you face situations that require these gifts. We have taken a few minutes to explore them, but I want to encourage you to delve into them more. If you don't know what they are, you won't use them. Knowing them is essential if you are going to activate them in your daily life.

WHAT YOU **CHOOSE** TO **THINK ABOUT** IS A **REALLY IMPORTANT CHOICE** YOU MAKE **EVERY DAY.**

GIFTS · OF · THE · SPIRIT

WISDOM
Understanding
COUNSEL
FORTITUDE
KNOWLEDGE
Piety
FEAR OF THE
LORD (REVERENCE)

 **STEP 4** **JOURNAL** ·

10 MIN

INSTRUCTIONS: Invite your class to open up to page 211 and take a few minutes in silence to journal their answers to those questions.

TIP

Take some time each week to journal in your workbook, answering the discussion questions and journal questions in more detail. Share with your class how this journaling is helping you become a better decision maker.

 **STEP 5** **ANNOUNCEMENTS** · · · · · · · · · · · · · · · · · ·

3 MIN

Tip

Encourage your class to attend youth group. It is a great way to connect them with the parish community. If they say it is lame, tell them to get involved and make it better.

Remind them you are praying for them. They need to hear this over and over again, every time you are with them.

Don't forget, it's not enough for them to see the short films once. Encourage the class to watch them again online or on the app.

STEP 6 CLOSING PRAYER

6 MIN

Pick a line from this session's Psalm and talk to them about why this line jumps out at you. This will help them anticipate and focus.

Begin with the Sign of the Cross before reading the Psalm slowly.

Close with a spontaneous prayer inviting God to help these young people open themselves up to the guidance of the Holy Spirit by learning to recognize his promptings in their daily lives.

Psalm 139

O LORD, thou hast searched me
and known me!

² Thou knowest when I sit down
and when I rise up; thou discernest
my thoughts from afar.

³ Thou searchest out my path and my lying
down, and art acquainted with all my ways.

⁴ Even before a word is on my tongue,
lo, O LORD, thou knowest it altogether.

⁵ Thou dost beset me behind and before,
and layest thy hand upon me.

⁶ Such knowledge is too wonderful for me;
it is high, I cannot attain it.

⁷ Whither shall I go from thy Spirit?
Or whither shall I flee from thy presence?

⁸ If I ascend to heaven, thou art there!
If I make my bed in Sheol, thou art there!

⁹ If I take the wings of the morning
and dwell in the uttermost parts of the sea,

¹⁰ even there thy hand shall lead me,
and thy right hand shall hold me.

¹¹ If I say, "Let only darkness cover me,
and the light about me be night,"

¹² even the darkness is not dark to thee,
the night is bright as the day;
for darkness is as light with thee.

¹³ For thou didst form my inward parts,
thou didst knit me together in
my mother's womb.

¹⁴ I praise thee, for thou art fearful and
wonderful. Wonderful are thy works!

Thou knowest me right well;
¹⁵ my frame was not hidden from thee,
when I was being made in secret, intricately
wrought in the depths of the earth.

¹⁶ Thy eyes beheld my unformed substance;
in thy book were written, every one of them,
the days that were formed for me,
when as yet there was none of them.

¹⁷ How precious to me are thy thoughts,
O God! How vast is the sum of them!

¹⁸ If I would count them, they are
more than the sand.
When I awake, I am still with thee.

¹⁹ O that thou wouldst slay the wicked,
O God, and that men of blood would
depart from me,²⁰ men who maliciously
defy thee, who lift themselves up
against thee for evil!

²¹ Do I not hate them that hate thee,
O LORD? And do I not loathe them
that rise up against thee?

²² I hate them with perfect hatred;
I count them my enemies.

²³ Search me, O God, and know my heart!
Try me and know my thoughts!

²⁴ And see if there be any wicked way in me,
and lead me in the way everlasting!

The CHURCH

Lord Jesus, you prayed that your people would be one; forgive us Lord and take away the pride and arrogance which divides your Church. Break down the walls which separate us; unite us with your bonds of love and accomplish your will. I pray that by the power of your Spirit your healing would work in the body of your Church and through me, to bring about the purpose of your will. Amen.

Author Unknown

QUICK SESSION OVERVIEW

STEP 1 | **WELCOME**
STEP 2 | **OPENING PRAYER**
STEP 3 | **ENGAGE – WATCH & DISCUSS**
STEP 4 | **JOURNAL**
STEP 5 | **ANNOUNCEMENTS**
STEP 6 | **CLOSING PRAYER**

SESSION NINE: THE CHURCH

Objectives:

- To demonstrate that there are lots of reasons to be proud to be Catholic.

- To teach candidates that the Church is part of God's plan for humanity.

- To help candidates recognize that the Church can play a powerful role in their lives, and that they play a unique and vital role in the mission of the Church.

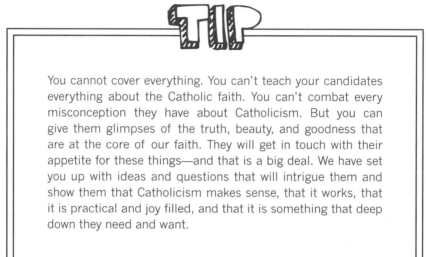

You cannot cover everything. You can't teach your candidates everything about the Catholic faith. You can't combat every misconception they have about Catholicism. But you can give them glimpses of the truth, beauty, and goodness that are at the core of our faith. They will get in touch with their appetite for these things—and that is a big deal. We have set you up with ideas and questions that will intrigue them and show them that Catholicism makes sense, that it works, that it is practical and joy filled, and that it is something that deep down they need and want.

LEADER GUIDE KEY

TIME-ICON: This icon serves as a guide to help you plan approximately how long each activity will take.

[WB5] This code serves as a reference to point you to the page in the Workbook where you can find the related activity/content.

Example: **[WB5]** *points you to page 5 in the Workbook*

The flag icon is the halfway mark and suggests a good breaking point if your program runs twenty-four classes (or approximately 60 minutes) instead of twelve 120 minute classes.

STEP 2 OPENING PRAYER ·························

You have probably already discovered that the hardest part of making this a powerful experience is classroom management.

You are in charge. Make sure your students know it. You don't need to scream and shout, but you do need to be firm, confident, and prepared.

If you cannot get them quiet and focused at the beginning, you will never get them quiet and focused. So take your time to get them settled before you begin.

3 MIN

Lord Jesus, you prayed that your people would be one; forgive us Lord and take away the pride and arrogance which divides your Church. Break down the walls which separate us; unite us with your bonds of love and accomplish your will. I pray that by the power of your Spirit your healing would work in the body of your Church and through me, to bring about the purpose of your will. Amen.

•———— *Author Unknown* ————•

STEP 3 ENGAGE: WATCH & DISCUSS

SESSION 9 INTRODUCTION

WATCH VIDEO

7 MIN

TIP:

We are all called to evangelize. You are doing just that by leading this group toward Confirmation. How can you encourage them to share the message with others? Invite them to share their favorite short film so far via their social media networks.

DISCUSSION QUESTION

4 MIN

1) What is the one idea in this short film that you found most helpful?

SESSION 9.1 THE FIRST CHRISTIANS AND THE EARLY CHURCH

WATCH VIDEO

7 MIN

9.1 THE FIRST CHRISTIANS & THE EARLY CHURCH

DISCUSSION QUESTIONS [WB219]

10 MIN

Tip

The first Christians were incredible. They literally changed the world. Make sure the candidates know how amazing the first century of Christianity was.

1) When you think of church, what comes to mind?

2) If you could ask a group of early Christians one question, what would you ask?

3) Why is it difficult to practice agape love?

EXERCISE

Invite a student to read aloud **"Who Was John Paul II?"** One of the extraordinary acts of his life was to forgive the man who shot and tried to kill him. Ask the candidates, "How hard do you think it was for John Paul II to forgive his shooter?" [WB229]

5 MIN

TIP!

Refusing to forgive somebody is like drinking poison and expecting the other person to die. Whom do you need to forgive? Whom do you need to ask forgiveness from?

HE WILL COME AGAIN IN GLORY TO JUDGE THE LIVING AND THE DEAD AND HIS KINGDOM WILL HAVE NO END. I BELIEVE IN THE HOLY SPIRIT, THE LORD, THE GIVER OF LIFE, WHO PROCEEDS FROM THE FATHER AND

"When we honestly ask ourselves which person in our lives means the most to us, we often find that it is those who, instead of giving advice, solutions, or cures, have chosen rather to share our pain and touch our wounds with a warm and tender hand. The friend who can be silent with us in a moment of despair or confusion, who can stay with us in an hour of grief and bereavement, who can tolerate not knowing, not curing, not healing and face with us the reality of our powerlessness, that is a friend who cares."

—Henri J. M. Nouwen

If you want to hear God laugh, tell him your plans!

9.3 The Good, The Bad, The Ugly & The Lies

The Good

For two thousand years wherever you find Catholics you find a group of people making phenomenal contributions to their local, national, and international communities. Every single day the Catholic Church feeds more people, houses more people, clothes more people, visits more imprisoned, cares for more sick people, and educates more people than any other institution on the planet.

The Church gave birth to scientific method, which has been at the center of scientific discovery for hundreds of years. The Church gave birth to the first university. The early Church was the first to institutionalize the care of widows, orphans, and the sick. The Church has also made incredible contributions in music, art, medicine, architecture, language, and law. In the area of law, equality before the law, trial by jury, and proof beyond a reasonable doubt are all the fruit of Catholic thought.

And no other organization or institution has done more than the Catholic Church in defending human rights around the world. The Catholic idea of charity—that we help those in need, without the expectation of anything in return, whether they are Catholic or not, and even if they despise us—is the idea of charity that even our secular society today strives to achieve.

In fact, all of these Catholic contributions spring from the notion of agape love. For two thousand years the Catholic Church has been a force for tremendous good in the world.

The Bad

There have also been some dark moments in our story. Our past is not perfect. Pope John Paul II made more than one hundred public apologies during his papacy on behalf of Catholics for events reaching back as far as one thousand years.

He apologized to women, Jews, minorities, people convicted by the Inquisition, Muslims killed by the Crusaders, and almost everyone who had suffered at the hands of the Catholic Church throughout history. He apologized for Catholics' involvement in the African slave trade, the Church's role in religious wars and burnings at the stake, and the legal process Galileo suffered. He apologized for injustices committed against women and the inactivity and silence of many Catholics during the Holocaust.

Our past is not without blemish. There have been some horrible moments in Catholic history. But it is important to recognize that these moments are the result of individuals wandering away from the teachings of Christ and his Church.

Here we find one of the central mysteries of God's plan: The Church is made up of human beings like you and me, who are in many ways weak and imperfect.

Some people look at the failings of the Church and use them as an excuse to leave. I see it very differently. All of the lowest moments in Church history are examples of what happens when we don't live the Catholic faith authentically. I have studied these low moments, and what I've found is immorality and personal weakness, selfishness and abuse of power. I've found Christ's teachings misunderstood and misrepresented. But the scandals that stain our history do not exist because we lived our Catholicism, but rather, because we failed to live it. And what I find most of all in the Church's history is a reflection of my own fragile and broken humanity.

When we behave as second-rate versions-of-ourselves bad things happen. That's true for us as individuals and it's true for the Church.

The Ugly

One of the ugliest scandals surrounding the Catholic Church is also one of the most recent: the sexual abuse scandal among priests. There is never any excuse for the abuse of a child. It is not only immoral and unchristian, but it is criminal in every civilized society. The abuse and the scandal were also mishandled in some cases by Church officials.

Scandals like this rock people's faith. When the Church fails to live up to her mission and the values she invites others to live by, the faith of millions of ordinary people is affected. Why? The Church is supposed to help people get closer to God. But when she gets caught up in a scandal it can stand as an obstacle between God and the people.

The first e-mail Pope John Paul II sent was an apology to everyone who had been abused by a priest or religious. Benedict XVI also apologized to the victims.

There have been some truly ugly moments in Catholic history. They are inexcusable. We should pray for the victims of these parts of our history.

Sometimes we have to suffer for the Church, just as Mary suffered watching her son being ridiculed and tortured.

WHO WAS John Paul II?

Saint John Paul II (1920–2005) was born in Poland. In 1978 he was elected the 264th Bishop of Rome. For the next twenty years he traveled the world tirelessly, bringing the hope, peace, and joy of the Gospel to everyone who would listen. He had a deep love for young people and out of love instituted World Youth Day. In 1981, Pope John Paul II was shot in St. Peter's Square. He survived the assassination attempt and visited his shooter in prison on Christmas in 1983. He is one of the modern giants of our faith. His story cannot be contained in a thousand pages. If you want to have a life-changing experience, read George Weigel's biography of Pope John Paul II, *Witness to Hope.*

SESSION 9.2 ONE, HOLY, CATHOLIC, AND APOSTOLIC

WATCH VIDEO

9 MIN

9.2 :One, Holy, Catholic, & Apostolic

This short film explores the Creed. Consider praying it together at the beginning of this video, and again at the end. This is a really practical way for them to understand how these lessons can change the way they think about Catholicism.

10 MIN

DISCUSSION QUESTIONS [WB225]

1) If Jesus wanted the Church to be one, why do you think there are so many different churches today?

2) How many popes have there been during your lifetime? Who were they? What do you remember about them?

3) What do you think was Jesus' main message?

SESSION 9.3 THE GOOD, THE BAD, THE UGLY, AND THE LIES

WATCH VIDEO

10 MIN

Many people who are good at leading are left-brain people. We like problems we can solve; we like answers; we like order; we like things to be in their place. But helping young people enter into a powerful relationship with Jesus and his Church can be messy. The path is different for every candidate. They all have different questions, struggles, doubts, and hopes. Be flexible. It's OK if every session does not go as you planned. Let the Holy Spirit guide you and these classes.

DISCUSSION QUESTIONS [WB232]

10 MIN

1) What makes you proudest to be Catholic?

2) In what ways has the Church disappointed you?

3) We all make mistakes, and we all sin against God. Do your own failings help you to understand why there have been scandals at different times in the history of the Church?

🕐 5 MIN

EXERCISE:

Tip

Read the class the list of the Seven Sacraments on page 234, and then ask them to debate this question: **How many sacraments can one person receive?**

I BELIEVE IN ONE, HOLY, CATHOLIC AND APOSTOLIC CHURCH. I CONFESS ONE BAPTISM FOR THE FORGIVENESS OF SINS AND I LOOK FORWARD TO THE RESURRECTION OF THE DEAD

7 SACRAMENTS ARE...

Baptism
EUCHARIST
confirmation
Reconciliation
ANOINTING of the SICK
marriage
Holy Orders

How many sacraments can one person receive?

9.4 Ten GREAT Reasons to be Catholic

I love being Catholic, and there are an infinite number of great reasons to be Catholic, but let's take a look at ten of them.

You can't put these things in order, and we could argue about the order until the end of the world. Be here they are:

10. This is the Church that Jesus Christ started and sent the Holy Spirit to guide. It is unique and original.

9. The Catholic Church has relieved more suffering than any other group of people in the history of the world. We care for the sick, the hungry, the lonely, the homeless, the uneducated, and the imprisoned. I love being part of that.

8. We have history and mystery. To really understand Christianity you need a historical perspective, and the history of Christianity is Catholic. For more than fifteen hundred years there were no Baptists, Methodists, Presbyterians, Anglicans, Pentecostal Christians, Lutherans, Mormons, Evangelical Christians, Non-Denominational Christians. Today, there are more than twenty-five thousand different Christian denominations, but they all lack the rich and beautiful history we have as Catholics. We have history, and we have mystery. We know it's all right not to have the answer to everything. Some things are a mystery, and that's OK.

7. We have the Saints. These are the great heroes and heroines of Christianity. They are the most diverse group of people in history. Some were rich and some were poor; some were very well educated and some had no formal education; some were young and others were old. They have lived in every century, on every continent, in every country – and they all tried to be the-best-version-of-themselves. Now they are in Heaven, cheering you on.

6. We believe in the power of prayer. At every moment of every day Mass is being prayed in thousands of places around the world. That's our family praying for the whole world. We don't just pray for Catholics; we pray for everyone. Imagine how different the history of the world would have been if the Catholic Church had never offered a single prayer.

5. It's the same all around the world. I took a group on a pilgrimage a few years ago and we all went to Mass in Florence. That night I asked the group about the experience of attending Mass in Italian. They said, "Even though I don't speak Italian, I still knew what was going on." Catholicism is the same everywhere, and that's a beautiful thing.

4. The Catholic Church is the premier defender of human rights.

3. You need to be part of something bigger than yourself. Life is not about you. It's about laying down your life in the service of others out of love for God. You could lay down your life for a sport, a career, money, things . . . and people do. But what a waste! The Catholic Church has the most important mission in the world—and you are invited to get involved and be a part of that great mission!

2. The Eucharist. Jesus Christ is truly present in the Eucharist.

1. You don't say no to God when he invites you. There are some invitations we don't turn down.

I can come up with great reasons to be Catholic all day long, but ultimately you need to come up with your own. I can't give you my love of the Church. I wish I could. In the end you have to make Catholicism your own.

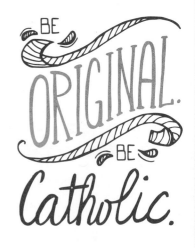

BE ORIGINAL. BE Catholic.

SESSION 9.4 TEN GREAT REASONS TO BE CATHOLIC

WATCH VIDEO

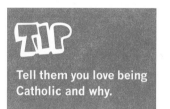

TIP

Tell them you love being Catholic and why.

4 MIN

DISCUSSION QUESTIONS [WB236]

10 MIN

1) What do you think is the best reason to be Catholic?

2) What did you learn in this session that really made you stop and think?

3) How did the top ten reasons to be Catholic change the way you view Catholicism?

EXERCISE VIRTUE IN FOCUS

TIP

5 MIN

This session highlights the virtue of faithfulness. Invite a candidate to read aloud the **Virtue in Focus** section. Choose one of the questions from the section and encourage the candidates to share their answers. [WB230]

WHO PROCEEDS FROM THE FATHER AND THE SON, WHO WITH THE FATHER AND THE SON IS ADORED AND GLORIFIED, WHO HAS SPOKEN THROUGH THE PROPHETS. I BELIEVE IN O

What would it be like if Mary was in your parish?

VIRTUE IN FOCUS

Faith·ful·ness
[feyth-*fuh*l-ness]

loyalty, constancy, and steadfastness

What are you faithful to?

Who is the most faithful person you know?

What can you do to increase your faith?

The Lies

History is also full of lies about the Catholic Church. These lies are often perpetuated by modern popular culture. Let's take a look at some.

One lie is the idea that the Church is against science and wants to keep everyone ignorant so they can be controlled. This is nonsense. Many of the great scientific discoveries were made by Catholic priests. And if the Church wanted to keep everyone ignorant why did it develop universities and become the champion of education for the common man?

Another lie that is perpetuated about the Church is that it is opposed to progress and is an obstacle to progress. This is also an absurd lie. The Church has been a champion of progress from the very beginning, and this is a tradition that has continued throughout our rich history of contribution. The Catholic Church has nurtured and encouraged progress in education, law, art, music, architecture, science, philosophy, theology, language, and human rights. In fact, many of the best minds of our times believe that Western civilization is almost completely indebted to the Catholic Church.

Today one of the biggest lies surrounds the priesthood. The media would have you believe that every priest sexually abuses children. In a recent poll, when asked what percentage of priests were pedophiles, respondents said between 33 and 50 percent. In fact, 1.8 percent of priests were involved in the scandal. The great majority of priests are good men who have given their lives to help you and me grow spiritually, become the-best-version-of-ourselves, and get to Heaven.

The world tends to ignore the goodness of the Church and blow our mistakes out of proportion to make them all-encompassing. At the beginning of this section we talked about some of the Church's great contributions—how many of those did you already know about? I've met many Catholics who didn't know any of those things.

The last lie I want to explore briefly with you is the idea that the Church is always behind the times. Not so. It is easy to present the Church as being old-fashioned and out of date, but this is a lie. The Church is a prophet and as such is ahead of the times.

One modern example of this can be found in the papal encyclical "Humanae Vitae." In it Pope Paul VI explained what would happen if artificial contraceptives became widely used in society. It was written in 1968, before you and I were born. It was written in a time very different from the world we live in today. But it is full of prophecy, and what Paul VI predicted would happen is exactly what has happened.

Pope Paul VI predicted artificial contraception would be bad for marriage, bad for families, and in particular, that it would lead to the objectification of women.

He was an unwelcome prophet of his times, and remains an unwelcome prophet in our times—but he is modern proof that the Church is ahead of the times, not behind the times.

The bottom line is this: Don't believe everything you hear about the Church. When someone criticizes the Church, ask them to prove it. If you have doubts about something, delve into the issue yourself so that you can really understand the great history of the Catholic Church. It is not a perfect history, but the Church has always been a force for incredible good in the world.

There have been some regrettable moments in the life of the Catholic Church, but a fair look at history demonstrates that violence and abuse are not the overarching story of Catholicism. Our story is primarily one of agape love, incredible contribution, and the relief of human suffering.

I'm proud to be Catholic, and the more I learn about our history, the prouder I become.

how wiLL **YOU** serve the Church?

WATCH VIDEO

9.5 DECISION point

Tip

Tell them something you learned from this session that you didn't know before.

2 MIN

EXERCISE: Know It. Think About It. Live It.

TIP

Ask someone to read aloud the Bible passage highlighted in the section **KNOW IT. THINK ABOUT IT. LIVE IT.** Ask another student to read the text from the workbook. [WB216]

Discuss with the class how they think they could share their talents with the Church to make it better for everyone.

5 MIN

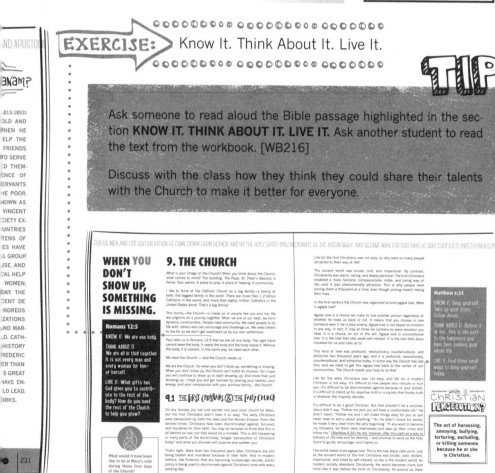

WHEN YOU DON'T SHOW UP, SOMETHING IS MISSING.

9. THE CHURCH

What is your image of the Church? When you think about the Church, what comes to mind? The building. The Pope. St. Peter's Basilica in Rome. Your parish. A place to pray. A place of healing. A community.

I like to think of the Catholic Church as a big family—a family of faith; the biggest family in the world. There are more than 1.2 billion Catholics in the world, and more than eighty million Catholics in the United States alone. That's a big family!

This family—the Church—is made up of people like you and me. We are pilgrims on a journey together. When we are at our best, we form dynamic communities. People need community. We need people to do life with, others who can encourage and challenge us. We need others to live for so we don't get swallowed up by our own selfishness.

Romans 12:5

KNOW IT: We are one body.

THINK ABOUT IT: We are all in this together. It is not every man and every woman for himself or herself.

LIVE IT: What gifts has God given you to contribute to the rest of the body? How do you need the rest of the Church to help you grow?

Paul tells us in Romans 12:5 that we are all one body. The right hand cannot leave the body. It needs the body and the body needs it. Without the body, it is useless. In the same way, we need each other.

We need the Church — and the Church needs us.

We are the Church. So when you don't show up, something is missing. When you don't show up, the Church can't fulfill its mission. So I hope you will continue to show up or start showing up. And more than just showing up, I hope you will get involved by sharing your talents, your energy, and your compassion with your spiritual family – the Church.

9.1 THE FIRST CHRISTIANS & THE EARLY CHURCH

On any Sunday you can just wander into your local church for Mass, but the first Christians didn't have it so easy. The early Christians were persecuted by both the Jews and the Roman Empire. From the earliest times, Christians have been discriminated against, tortured, and murdered for their faith. You may be tempted to think that this is all behind us now, but that would be a mistake. This is still happening in many parts of the world today. Google "persecution of Christians today" and what you discover will surprise and sadden you.

That's right. More than two thousand years later, Christians are still being beaten and murdered because of their faith. And in modern nations, like America, that are becoming increasingly secular, public policy is being used to discriminate against Christians with every passing day.

What would it have been like to be at Mary's side during those first days of the Church?

Life for the first Christians was not easy, so why were so many people attracted to their way of life?

The ancient world was brutal, cold, and impersonal. By contrast, Christianity was warm, caring, and deeply personal. The first Christians modeled a more humane, compassionate, noble, and loving way of life—and it was phenomenally attractive. This is why people were joining them a thousand at a time, even though joining meant risking their lives.

In the first century the Church was organized around agape love. What is agape love?

Agape love is a choice we make to love another person regardless of whether he loves us back or not. It means that you choose to love someone even if he is your enemy. Agape love is not based on emotion in any way. In fact, it may at times be contrary to every emotion you feel. It is a choice, an act of the will. Agape love is unconditional love. It is the love that sets aside self-interest. It is the love that Jesus modeled for us and calls us to.

This kind of love was profound, revolutionary, countercultural, and attractive two thousand years ago, and it is profound, revolutionary, countercultural, and attractive today in some way the Church has lost this, and we need to get this agape love back at the center of our communities. The Church needs your help to do that.

Life for the early Christians was not easy, and life for a modern Christian is not easy. It's difficult to love people who ridicule or hurt you. It's difficult to be discriminated against because of your beliefs. It's difficult to stand up for objective truth in a society that thinks truth is whatever the majority decides.

It's difficult to be a good Christian. But that shouldn't be a surprise. Jesus didn't say, "Follow me and you will have a comfortable life." He didn't teach, "Follow me and I will make things easy for you so you never have to worry about anything." No, he didn't mince his words; he made it very clear from the very beginning: "If any want to become my followers, let them deny themselves and take up their cross and follow me." (Matthew 6:24) He did, however, offer this path as a way to fullness of life now and for eternity – and promise to send us the Holy Spirit to guide, encourage, and inspire us.

The world needs more agape love. This is the love Jesus calls us to. Just as the ancient world of the first Christians was brutal, cold, distant, impersonal, and ruled by self-interest, so too is the modern world. As modern society abandons Christianity, the world becomes more and more like it was before the birth of Christianity. All around us there

Matthew 6:24

KNOW IT: Deny yourself. Take up your cross. Follow Jesus.

THINK ABOUT IT: Believe it or not, this is the path to the happiness you have been seeking your whole life.

LIVE IT: Find three small ways to deny yourself today.

What is **CHRISTIAN PERSECUTION?**

The act of harassing, annoying, bullying, torturing, excluding, or killing someone because he or she is Christian.

231

7 MIN

INSTRUCTIONS: It's time to journal. This time is sacred; remind them of that. Invite your class to open up to page 239 and take a few minutes in silence to journal their answers to those questions.

TIP

Lead by example. The questions being posed throughout these sessions are life's biggest questions. Take some time to grapple with them. Let the candidates know that you are still grappling with them . . . but the grappling is worth it.

STEP 5 **ANNOUNCEMENTS**

3 MIN

Tip

Thank them for coming.

Remind them you are praying for them. Ask them if there is anything in particular they want you to pray for this week.

Encourage them to watch the short films again during the week online or on the app.

STEP 6 CLOSING PRAYER

4 MIN

TiP

Before you read the Psalm today, encourage your class to sit still and quiet for a couple of minutes and just listen to whatever God is saying to them.

Close with a spontaneous prayer inviting God in, thanking him for giving us the Church, and asking him to help us appreciate it more with every passing day.

Psalm 16

Preserve me, O God, for in thee I take refuge.
² I say to the Lord, "Thou art my Lord;
I have no good apart from thee."

³ As for the saints in the land, they are the noble,
in whom is all my delight.

⁴ Those who choose another god multiply their sorrows;
their libations of blood I will not pour out
or take their names upon my lips.
⁵ The Lord is my chosen portion and my cup;
thou holdest my lot.
⁶ The lines have fallen for me in pleasant places;
yea, I have a goodly heritage.

⁷ I bless the Lord who gives me counsel;
in the night also my heart instructs me.

⁸ I keep the Lord always before me;
because he is at my right hand, I shall not be moved.

⁹ Therefore my heart is glad, and my soul rejoices;
my body also dwells secure.

¹⁰ For thou dost not give me up to Sheol,
or let thy godly one see the Pit.

¹¹ Thou dost show me the path of life;
in thy presence there is fulness of joy,
in thy right hand are pleasures for evermore.

226 | DECISION POINT ....▶ THE CHURCH ○○○

CONFIRMATION

Lord, make me an instrument of your peace; where there is hatred, let me sow love; where there is injury, pardon; where there is error, truth; where there is doubt, faith; where there is despair, hope; where there is darkness, light; and where there is sadness, joy.

O Divine Master, grant that I may not so much seek to be consoled as to console; to be understood as to understand; to be loved as to love. For it is in giving that we receive; it is in pardoning that we are pardoned; and it is in dying that we are born to eternal life. Amen.

St. Francis of Assisi

QUICK SESSION OVERVIEW

STEP 1 WELCOME

STEP 2 OPENING PRAYER

STEP 3 ENGAGE – WATCH & DISCUSS

STEP 4 JOURNAL

STEP 5 ANNOUNCEMENTS

STEP 6 CLOSING PRAYER

SESSION TEN: CONFIRMATION

Objectives:

- To demonstrate that candidates are personally called and chosen by God, but they are responsible for how they respond to that call.

- To teach candidates how to prepare to receive the sacrament of Confirmation.

- To help candidates recognize that Confirmation is not the end of something, but the beginning of an incredible new phase in their faith journey.

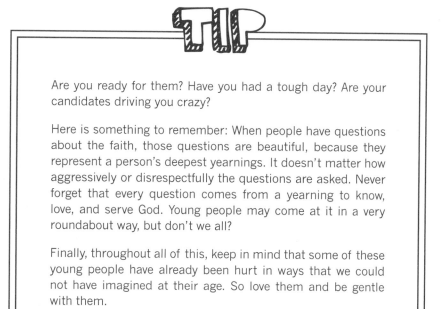

Are you ready for them? Have you had a tough day? Are your candidates driving you crazy?

Here is something to remember: When people have questions about the faith, those questions are beautiful, because they represent a person's deepest yearnings. It doesn't matter how aggressively or disrespectfully the questions are asked. Never forget that every question comes from a yearning to know, love, and serve God. Young people may come at it in a very roundabout way, but don't we all?

Finally, throughout all of this, keep in mind that some of these young people have already been hurt in ways that we could not have imagined at their age. So love them and be gentle with them.

LEADER GUIDE KEY

TIME-ICON: This icon serves as a guide to help you plan approximately how long each activity will take.

[WB5] This code serves as a reference to point you to the page in the Workbook where you can find the related activity/content.

Example: **[WB5]** *points you to page 5 in the Workbook*

The flag icon is the halfway mark and suggests a good breaking point if your program runs twenty-four classes (or approximately 60 minutes) instead of twelve 120 minute classes.

Tip

How many candidates are in your class? How many of them believe that you want what is best for them? Have you convinced them that you have their best interests at heart?

We respect and listen to people we believe have our best interests at heart. If you have not won them in this way yet, ask yourself why.

3 MIN

Lord, make me an instrument of your peace; where there is hatred, let me sow love; where there is injury, pardon; where there is error, truth; where there is doubt, faith; where there is despair, hope; where there is darkness, light; and where there is sadness, joy.

O Divine Master, grant that I may not so much seek to be consoled as to console; to be understood as to understand; to be loved as to love. For it is in giving that we receive; it is in pardoning that we are pardoned; and it is in dying that we are born to eternal life. Amen.

— *St. Francis of Assisi* —

STEP 3 ENGAGE: WATCH & DISCUSS

SESSION 10 INTRODUCTION

WATCH VIDEO

IF YOU GET THE
MAN RIGHT

4 MIN

TIP:

The day of Confirmation is quickly approaching. Mention it from time to time. Tell them you are excited for them. Throughout this process, take a moment in each class to build anticipation.

DISCUSSION QUESTION

6 MIN

1) What is the one idea in this short film that you found most helpful?

SESSION 10.1 WHAT IS CONFIRMATION?

WATCH VIDEO

5 MIN

10.1 WHAT IS CONFIRMATION?

DISCUSSION QUESTIONS [WB246]

10 MIN

Tip Nothing brings people to Jesus like joy. Let your students see the joy in your life. Make sure they know that you are happiest when you are walking with God.

1) Do you believe that God has good plans for you?

2) What can you do to find out the plans God has for your future?

3) How has your idea of Confirmation changed since we began our time together?

EXERCISE

Invite a student to read aloud **"Who Was John the Baptist?"**
Discuss how we can prepare the way for Jesus in the world today.
[WB260]

6 MIN

TIP! People don't do anything until they are inspired, but once they are inspired there is almost nothing they will not do. How does John the Baptist inspire you? How can you share that inspiration with the candidates?

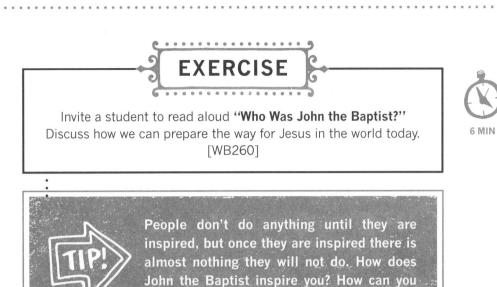

AND ROSE AGAIN ON THE THIRD DAY IN ACCORDANCE WITH THE SCRIPTURES. HE ASCENDED INTO HEAVEN

After a short prayer the bishop will invite you and your sponsor to come before him for the **Laying on of hands and Anointing with chrism.** Your sponsor will place his or her hand on your right shoulder, you or your sponsor will tell the bishop your Confirmation name, then the bishop will trace the sign of the cross on your forehead with the sacred oil chrism and say, "Be sealed with the Gift of the Holy Spirit." You respond, "Amen." Then the bishop will extend to you a sign of peace, saying, "Peace be with you." You respond, "And with your spirit."

After all the candidates have stood before the bishop, the Mass continues with the **General Intercessions.** This is that time in the Mass when we pray for all the needs of every member of the community, and for the whole world.

You will experience a special unity as we pray together the **Lord's Prayer,** offer each other a **Sign of Peace,** and receive **Holy Communion.**

The bishop will then bring the Mass to a close with a **Solemn Blessing** and send you into the world to witness to God's love by living out the mission he has entrusted to you.

I want to encourage you in a special way to be mindful of that moment when the bishop lays his hands on you and anoints you with the chrism. That is going to be one of the most powerful moments of your life. Focus in that moment and ask God to open your heart, mind, and soul to every good thing he wants to bestow upon you.

How would you act differently if Mary was sitting next to you in class this week?

WHO WAS John the Baptist?

John the Baptist was an itinerant preacher and one of the great religious figures of all time. Jesus and John the Baptist were cousins, through their mothers, Mary and Elizabeth. John was the child who danced for joy in Elizabeth's womb when Mary visited, which we remember in the Second Joyful Mystery of the Rosary (Luke 1:39–56). John challenged people to repent, to turn away from their sinful and selfish ways and turn back to God (Matthew 3:1–17). John's mission was to prepare the way for Jesus. What's your mission? We celebrate John the Baptist with two feast days: June 24 (birth) and August 29 (death).

DISCUSSION QUESTIONS

1. IF YOU COULD ASK THE BISHOP ONE QUESTION, WHAT WOULD YOU ASK?

2. ARE YOU NERVOUS ABOUT YOUR CONFIRMATION?

3. HOW ARE YOU PREPARING FOR CONFIRMATION?

260 **DECISION POINT**

CONFIRMATION 261

SESSION 10.2 **THE POWER OF PREPARATION**

6 MIN

WATCH VIDEO

10.2 THE POWER OF PREPARATION

▶

TIP

Before starting the short film, ask the students what they feel they have prepared for well in the past. Sporting event? Exam? Vacation?

---

10 MIN

DISCUSSION QUESTIONS [WB251]

1) What event in your life have you prepared for more than any other?

2) Who have been your spiritual coaches and mentors throughout your life?

3) How has the way you pray and what you pray for changed over the past few months?

SESSION 10.3 HOW WILL CONFIRMATION CHANGE YOU?

WATCH VIDEO

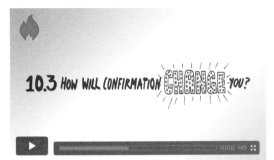

6 MIN

Keeping control of the group can be the biggest challenge as a leader. If you find yourself yelling, you have probably lost control of the class—and they know it. One of the best ways to keep control is to prepare well before you arrive. Preparation breeds confidence.

DISCUSSION QUESTIONS [WB256]

10 MIN

1) In what practical ways do you think Confirmation will change you?

2) Which of the seven gifts of the Holy Spirit could you most use at this time in your life?

3) When did you last pray to the Holy Spirit, asking for help to make a decision?

6 MIN

EXERCISE:

> ### Tip
>
> The day itself. Talk about the day they will be confirmed. Ask them how they are feeling about it. Just talk with them. Some will be nervous. Some will be hesitant. Some are only doing it because their parents want them to. Some don't want to be confirmed. But just talk to them and let them talk about how they are feeling. Sometimes we need to say something just to get it off our hearts—and just saying it brings us new perspective.

the BEST VERSION OF YOURSELF

SESSION 10.4 **ON THE DAY**

WATCH VIDEO

Tell them about your Confirmation. Make sure you know the exact date. That signals to them that it is important and memorable.

6 MIN

DISCUSSION QUESTIONS [WB261]

10 MIN

1) If you could ask the Bishop one question, what would you ask?

2) Are you nervous about your Confirmation?

3) How are you preparing for Confirmation?

EXERCISE — VIRTUE IN FOCUS

6 MIN

> **TIP**
>
> This session highlights the virtue of modesty. Invite someone to read aloud the **Virtue in Focus** section. Choose one of the questions from the section and encourage the candidates to share their answers. [WB259]

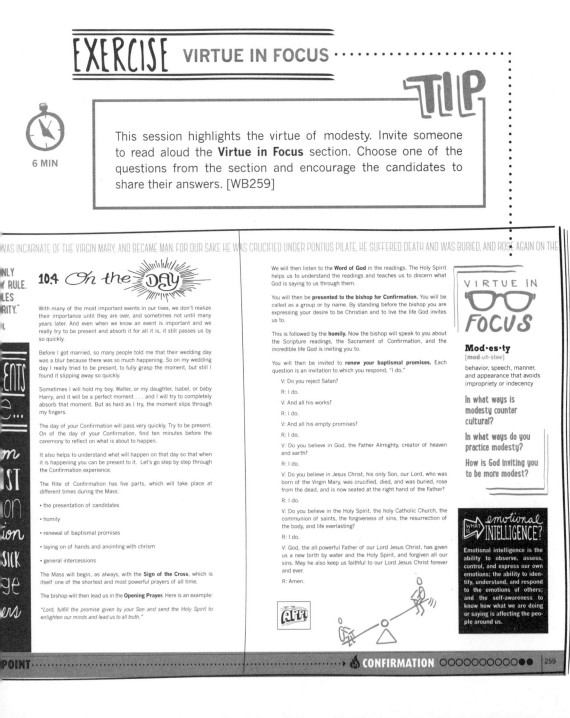

WAS INCARNATE OF THE VIRGIN MARY, AND BECAME MAN. FOR OUR SAKE HE WAS CRUCIFIED UNDER PONTIUS PILATE, HE SUFFERED DEATH AND WAS BURIED, AND ROSE AGAIN ON THE

10.4 On the DAY

With many of the most important events in our lives, we don't realize their importance until they are over, and sometimes not until many years later. And even when we know an event is important and we really try to be present and absorb it for all it is, it still passes us by so quickly.

Before I got married, so many people told me that their wedding day was a blur because there was so much happening. So on my wedding day I really tried to be present, to fully grasp the moment, but still I found it slipping away so quickly.

Sometimes I will hold my boy, Walter, or my daughter, Isabel, or baby Harry, and it will be a perfect moment . . . and I will try to completely absorb that moment. But as hard as I try, the moment slips through my fingers.

The day of your Confirmation will pass very quickly. Try to be present. On of the day of your Confirmation, find ten minutes before the ceremony to reflect on what is about to happen.

It also helps to understand what will happen on that day so that when it is happening you can be present to it. Let's go step by step through the Confirmation experience.

The Rite of Confirmation has five parts, which will take place at different times during the Mass:

- the presentation of candidates
- homily
- renewal of baptismal promises
- laying on of hands and anointing with chrism
- general intercessions

The Mass will begin, as always, with the **Sign of the Cross**, which is itself one of the shortest and most powerful prayers of all time.

The bishop will then lead us in the **Opening Prayer**. Here is an example:

"Lord, fulfill the promise given by your Son and send the Holy Spirit to enlighten our minds and lead us to all truth."

We will then listen to the **Word of God** in the readings. The Holy Spirit helps us to understand the readings and teaches us to discern what God is saying to us through them.

You will then be **presented to the bishop for Confirmation.** You will be called as a group or by name. By standing before the bishop you are expressing your desire to be Christian and to live the life God invites us to.

This is followed by the **homily.** Now the bishop will speak to you about the Scripture readings, the Sacrament of Confirmation, and the incredible life God is inviting you to.

You will then be invited to **renew your baptismal promises.** Each question is an invitation to which you respond, "I do."

V: Do you reject Satan?

R: I do.

V: And all his works?

R: I do.

V: And all his empty promises?

R: I do.

V: Do you believe in God, the Father Almighty, creator of heaven and earth?

R: I do.

V: Do you believe in Jesus Christ, his only Son, our Lord, who was born of the Virgin Mary, was crucified, died, and was buried, rose from the dead, and is now seated at the right hand of the Father?

R: I do.

V: Do you believe in the Holy Spirit, the holy Catholic Church, the communion of saints, the forgiveness of sins, the resurrection of the body, and life everlasting?

R: I do.

V: God, the all-powerful Father of our Lord Jesus Christ, has given us a new birth by water and the Holy Spirit, and forgiven all our sins. May he also keep us faithful to our Lord Jesus Christ forever and ever.

R: Amen.

VIRTUE IN FOCUS

Mod·es·ty
[mod-uh-stee]

behavior, speech, manner, and appearance that avoids impropriety or indecency

In what ways is modesty counter cultural?

In what ways do you practice modesty?

How is God inviting you to be more modest?

WHAT emotional INTELLIGENCE?

Emotional intelligence is the ability to observe, assess, control, and express our own emotions; the ability to identify, understand, and respond to the emotions of others; and the self-awareness to know how what we are doing or saying is affecting the people around us.

WATCH VIDEO

Tip

Remind them that Confirmation is a big deal whether or not they realize that yet.

3 MIN

EXERCISE: Know It. Think About It. Live It.

TIP

Ask someone to read aloud the Bible passage highlighted in the section **KNOW IT. THINK ABOUT IT. LIVE IT.** Ask another student to read the text from the workbook. [WB264]

Invite the class to sit still and quiet for two minutes and reflect on whom or what they are serving.

5 MIN

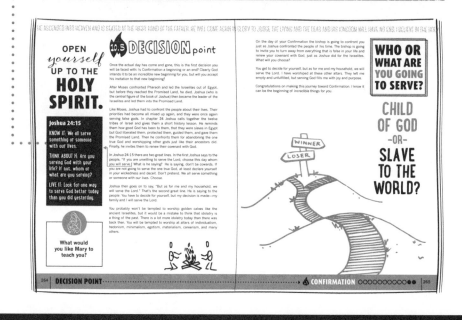

HE ASCENDED INTO HEAVEN AND IS SEATED AT THE RIGHT HAND OF THE FATHER. HE WILL COME AGAIN IN GLORY TO JUDGE THE LIVING AND THE DEAD AND HIS KINGDOM WILL HAVE NO END. I BELIEVE IN THE HOLY

OPEN *yourself* **UP TO THE HOLY SPIRIT.**

10.5 DECISION point

Once the actual day has come and gone, this is the first decision you will be faced with: Is Confirmation a beginning or an end? Clearly God intends it to be an incredible new beginning for you, but will you accept his invitation to that new beginning?

After Moses confronted Pharaoh and led the Israelites out of Egypt, but before they reached the Promised Land, he died. Joshua (who is the central figure of the book of Joshua) then became the leader of the Israelites and led them into the Promised Land.

Like Moses, Joshua had to confront the people about their lives. Their priorities had become all mixed up again, and they were once again serving false gods. In chapter 24 Joshua calls together the twelve tribes of Israel and gives them a short history lesson. He reminds them how good God has been to them, that they were slaves in Egypt but God liberated them, protected them, guided them, and gave them the Promised Land. Then he confronts them for abandoning the one true God and worshipping other gods just like their ancestors did. Finally, he invites them to renew their covenant with God.

In Joshua 24:15 there are two great lines. In the first Joshua says to the people, "If you are unwilling to serve the Lord, choose this day whom you will serve." What is he saying? He is saying, Don't be cowards. If you are not going to serve the one true God, at least declare yourself in your wickedness and deceit. Don't pretend. We all serve something or someone with our lives. Choose.

Joshua then goes on to say, "But as for me and my household, we will serve the Lord." That's the second great line. He is saying to the people: You have to decide for yourself, but my decision is made—my family and I will serve the Lord.

You probably won't be tempted to worship golden calves like the ancient Israelites, but it would be a mistake to think that idolatry is a thing of the past. There is a lot more idolatry today than there was back then. You will be tempted to worship at altars of individualism, hedonism, minimalism, egotism, materialism, careerism, and many others.

Joshua 24:15

KNOW IT: We all serve something or someone with our lives.

THINK ABOUT IT: Are you serving God with your life? If not, whom or what are you serving?

LIVE IT: Look for one way to serve God better today than you did yesterday.

What would you like Mary to teach you?

On the day of your Confirmation the bishop is going to confront you just as Joshua confronted the people of his time. The bishop is going to invite you to turn away from everything that is false in your life and renew your covenant with God, just as Joshua did for the Israelites. What will you choose?

You get to decide for yourself, but as for me and my household, we will serve the Lord. I have worshipped at these other altars. They left me empty and unfulfilled, but serving God fills me with joy and purpose.

Congratulations on making this journey toward Confirmation. I know it can be the beginning of incredible things for you.

WHO OR WHAT ARE YOU GOING TO SERVE?

CHILD OF GOD –OR– SLAVE TO THE WORLD?

WINNER
LOSER

264 **DECISION POINT**

CONFIRMATION 265

STEP 4 JOURNAL ···································

10 MIN

INSTRUCTIONS: It's time to journal. This time is sacred; remind them of that. Invite your class to open up to page 266 and take a few minutes in silence to journal their answers to those questions.

TIP

Tell them you wish you had taken these types of things more seriously when you were their age, and that you could have avoided a lot of challenges and heartache if you had. Tell them that you wish there was a program as good as this when you were being confirmed.

STEP 5 ANNOUNCEMENTS ···············

3 MIN

Tip

Thank them for coming. Never stop thanking them for coming.

Tell them you enjoyed your time with them. Identify a moment in the class that you thought was particularly powerful.

Remind them you are praying for them.

Encourage them to watch the short films again during the week online or on the app.

STEP 6   CLOSING PRAYER ·

TIP

Before you read the Psalm today, encourage your class to sit still and quiet for a couple of minutes and just listen to whatever God is saying to them.

Close with a spontaneous prayer asking God to bless these young people in their journey toward Confirmation and to fill them with courage to continue to do the next right thing and choose the path that God is inviting them to walk.

5 MIN

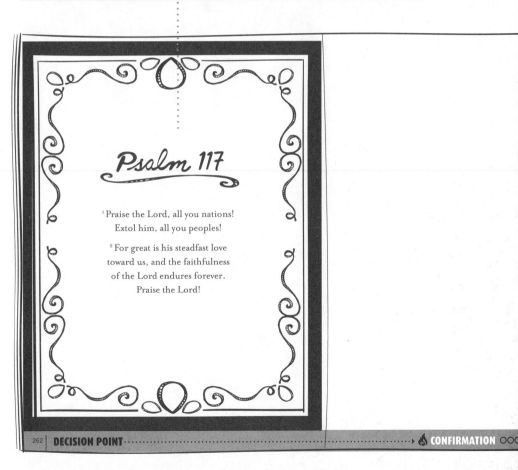

Psalm 117

¹ Praise the Lord, all you nations!
Extol him, all you peoples!

² For great is his steadfast love
toward us, and the faithfulness
of the Lord endures forever.
Praise the Lord!

Made for

MISSION

Lord, teach me to be generous. Teach me to serve you as you deserve; to give and not to count the cost, to fight and not to heed the wounds, to toil and not to seek for rest, to labor and not to ask for reward, save that of knowing that I do your will. Amen.

St Ignatius

QUICK SESSION OVERVIEW

STEP 1 WELCOME
STEP 2 OPENING PRAYER
STEP 3 ENGAGE – WATCH & DISCUSS
STEP 4 JOURNAL
STEP 5 ANNOUNCEMENTS
STEP 6 CLOSING PRAYER

SESSION ELEVEN: MADE FOR MISSION

Objectives:

- To demonstrate that when people abandon God and his ways, the world becomes a mess.

- To teach candidates that God created them on purpose and for a purpose.

- To help candidates discover the mission God is calling them to.

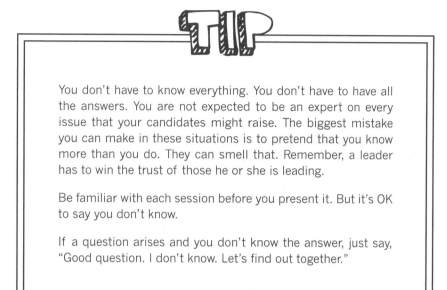

TIP

You don't have to know everything. You don't have to have all the answers. You are not expected to be an expert on every issue that your candidates might raise. The biggest mistake you can make in these situations is to pretend that you know more than you do. They can smell that. Remember, a leader has to win the trust of those he or she is leading.

Be familiar with each session before you present it. But it's OK to say you don't know.

If a question arises and you don't know the answer, just say, "Good question. I don't know. Let's find out together."

✳ LEADER GUIDE KEY

⊘ **TIME-ICON: This icon serves as a guide to help you plan approximately how long each activity will take.**

[WB5] **This code serves as a reference to point you to the page in the Workbook where you can find the related activity/ content.**

Example: **[WB5]** *points you to page 5 in the Workbook*

⚑ **The flag icon is the halfway mark and suggests a good breaking point if your program runs twenty-four classes (or approximately 60 minutes) instead of twelve 120 minute classes.**

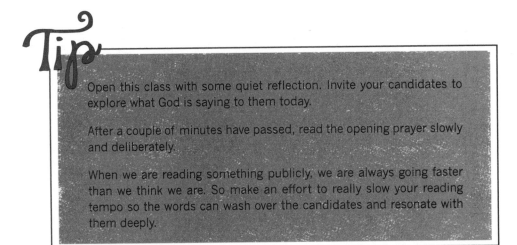

Tip

Open this class with some quiet reflection. Invite your candidates to explore what God is saying to them today.

After a couple of minutes have passed, read the opening prayer slowly and deliberately.

When we are reading something publicly, we are always going faster than we think we are. So make an effort to really slow your reading tempo so the words can wash over the candidates and resonate with them deeply.

3 MIN

Lord, teach me to be generous. Teach me to serve you as you deserve; to give and not to count the cost, to fight and not to heed the wounds, to toil and not to seek for rest, to labor and not to ask for reward, save that of knowing that I do your will. Amen.

— *St Ignatius* —

STEP 3 ENGAGE: WATCH & DISCUSS

SESSION 11 INTRODUCTION

WATCH VIDEO

6 MIN

> **TIP:** The world is a mess. Everyone knows it. This film explains how we can change the world. Too often we throw our hands up helplessly because we fall into the trap of believing that the world's problems are so big that there is nothing we can do. But we can do something.

DISCUSSION QUESTION

6 MIN

1) What is the one idea in this short film that you found most helpful?

SESSION 11.1 THE WORLD IS A MESS

WATCH VIDEO

7 MIN

DISCUSSION QUESTIONS [WB273]

10 MIN

Tip   At different times in our lives we all feel called to mission. Some missions are large and some are small. Talk to your class about how and why you felt called to lead them to Confirmation.

1) In what ways do you think the world is a mess?

2) How do you sense God is calling you to make the world a better place?

3) What's one thing you can do today that will make the world a better place?

EXERCISE

🕑 **5 MIN**

Invite a student to read aloud **"Who Was John Henry Newman?"** Every year millions of people around the world convert from other faiths to become Catholic. Discuss with your candidates what they think attracts these people to Catholicism. [WB282]

> **TIP!**
>
> Who is your favorite convert? Talk a little about this person and why you admire him or her.

I BELIEVE IN ONE GOD, THE FATHER ALMIGHTY, MAKER OF HEAVEN AND EARTH, OF ALL THINGS VISIBLE AND

desire, God wants us to get beyond our shallow desires, which are often selfish or pointless, and uncover the deepest desires of our hearts.

When I am the best version of myself, I say no to the doughnuts and I have a salad for lunch instead. To the world this is a simple choice between doughnuts and a salad. But as we grow spiritually, God shows us that there are many layers and dimensions to every decision.

On one level, yes, it's just a choice between doughnuts and a salad. On another level it's a choice between doughnuts and being healthy. That's a different perspective. On another level it's a choice between doughnuts and being alive when she gets married . . . to be alive to see her life unfold . . . and meet the person she will spend her life with . . . and meet my grandchildren. . . .

When we embrace God and his way of life, he reveals many dimensions of everyday life that we have never seen or thought about before. God is speaking to you through your deepest desires. Seek out your deepest desires for good things and have the courage to pursue them.

The most common preface to any sentence in the Bible is "God said . . ." God said to Adam, Noah, Moses, and Abraham. God spoke to everyone. It isn't that he has stopped speaking, but that humanity has stopped listening. God speaks to us in so many ways—through prayer, the Scriptures, the sacraments, through the life, teachings, and history of the Church; through other people, events, and circumstances.

You have been designed by God for a specific mission. This is what John Henry Newman wrote, "God has created me to do him some definite service. He has committed some work to me, which he has not committed to another. I have my mission." God has assigned a mission to you. If you don't fulfill your mission it will go undone. The world is a mess because too many people have abandoned their God-given mission.

Find your mission. It will change your life in the most wonderful ways . . . forever!

Who was JOHN HENRY NEWMAN?

JOHN HENRY NEWMAN (1801–1890) was one of the central religious figures in England in the nineteenth century. A respected academic, he was originally a priest in the Church of England and a leader in the Oxford Movement. This was an influential group of Anglicans who wanted to return the Church of England to many Catholic beliefs and practices. In 1845 Newman left the Church of England and was received in the Roman Catholic Church, where he was eventually appointed as cardinal by Pope Leo XIII. Unlike most saints, his feast day is not the day of his death, but rather the day of his conversion to Catholicism, September 19.

How can Mary help you find and live out your mission?

DISCUSSION

1. WHO DO YOU KNOW WHO HAS FOUND AND FOLLOWED THEIR MISSION IN LIFE?

2. HAVE YOU EVER ASKED GOD WHAT MISSION HE HAS FOR YOU?

3. HOW DO YOU THINK WHAT YOU WANT FOR YOURSELF IS DIFFERENT FROM WHAT GOD WANTS FOR YOU?

282 **DECISION POINT** .... ▶ **MADE FOR MISSION** ○○○○○○○○○○○● 283

SESSION 11.2 A WORLD WITHOUT NEIGHBORS

WATCH VIDEO

4 MIN

11.2 A WORLD *WITHOUT* NEIGHBORS

> If you ask someone a question and he or she is struggling to answer, pause for a moment; don't be afraid of the silence. But if you can tell the person needs time to think about it, ask, "Would you like me to come back to you?"

10 MIN

DISCUSSION QUESTIONS [WB278]

1) Jesus calls us to love our neighbor as we love ourselves. Whom do you consider to be your neighbor?

2) Why do you think so many children die from lack of food?

3) Are you willing to make sacrifices to reduce the amount of suffering in the world?

SESSION 11.3 FINDING YOUR MISSION

WATCH VIDEO

8 MIN

TIP

If you feel like the group needs a change, pair everyone with a partner. Ask them to discuss the questions together. Allow them enough time to share. Help pace them by letting them know when they should be moving on to the next question. Then ask the group to share something their partner said. People are much more willing to share their partner's answer.

DISCUSSION QUESTIONS [WB283]

10 MIN

1) Who do you know who has found and followed their mission in life?

2) Have you ever asked God what mission he has for you?

3) How do you think what you want for yourself is different from what God wants for you?

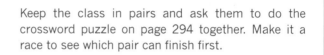

EXERCISE:

5 MIN

Tip

Keep the class in pairs and ask them to do the crossword puzzle on page 294 together. Make it a race to see which pair can finish first.

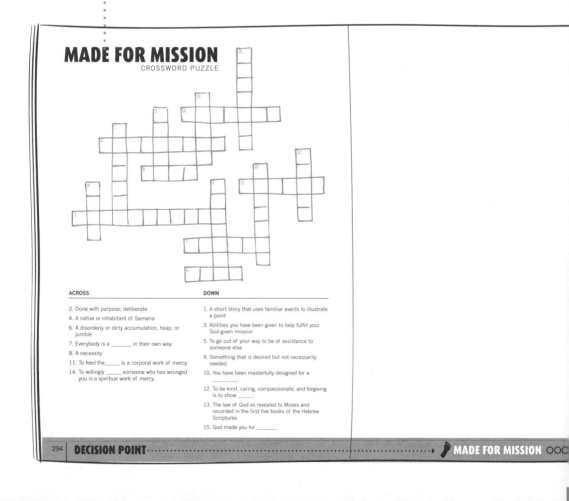

MADE FOR MISSION
CROSSWORD PUZZLE

ACROSS

2. Done with purpose; deliberate
4. A native or inhabitant of Samaria
6. A disorderly or dirty accumulation, heap, or jumble
7. Everybody is a _____ in their own way.
8. A necessity
11. To feed the_____ is a corporal work of mercy.
14. To willingly _____ someone who has wronged you is a spiritual work of mercy.

DOWN

1. A short story that uses familiar events to illustrate a point
3. Abilities you have been given to help fulfill your God-given mission
5. To go out of your way to be of assistance to someone else
9. Something that is desired but not necessarily needed
10. You have been masterfully designed for a _____.
12. To be kind, caring, compassionate, and forgiving is to show _____.
13. The law of God as revealed to Moses and recorded in the first five books of the Hebrew Scriptures
15. God made you for _____.

294 | **DECISION POINT** · ▶ **MADE FOR MISSION** ○○○

SESSION 11.4 **YOUR UNTAPPED GREATNESS**

WATCH VIDEO

 ·········

Loving our neighbor is among our primary Christian responsibilities. But how do we do that?

7 MIN

DISCUSSION QUESTIONS [WB289]

10 MIN

1) Who do you know who is great at serving other people?

2) What does the story about the rich man and Lazarus make you think about?

3) Do you think you will be happier if you find and follow your mission?

EXERCISE VIRTUE IN FOCUS

TIP

🕐 **5 MIN**

This session highlights the virtue of generosity. Invite someone to read aloud the **Virtue in Focus** section. Choose one of the questions from the section and encourage the candidates to share their answers. [WB292]

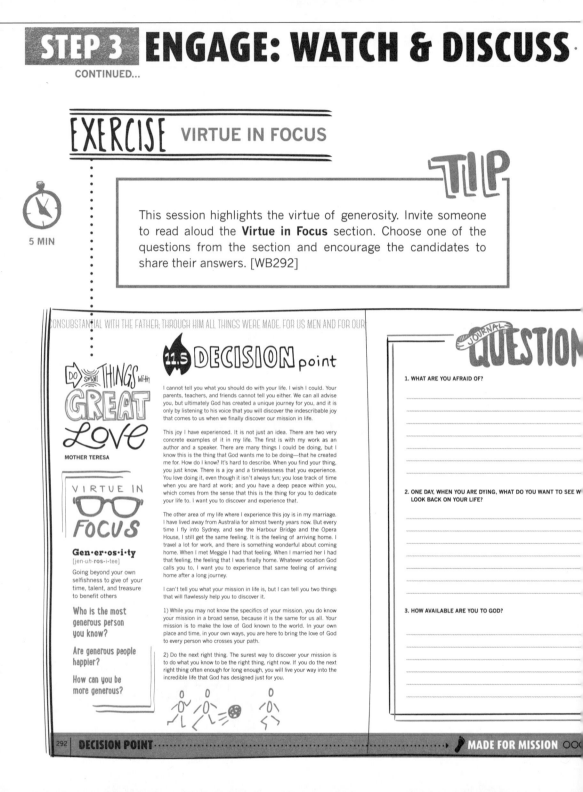

CONSUBSTANTIAL WITH THE FATHER; THROUGH HIM ALL THINGS WERE MADE. FOR US MEN AND FOR OUR

DO small THINGS with GREAT Love

MOTHER TERESA

VIRTUE IN FOCUS

Gen·er·os·i·ty
[jen-*uh*-**ros**-i-tee]

Going beyond your own selfishness to give of your time, talent, and treasure to benefit others

Who is the most generous person you know?

Are generous people happier?

How can you be more generous?

11.5 DECISION point

I cannot tell you what you should do with your life. I wish I could. Your parents, teachers, and friends cannot tell you either. We can all advise you, but ultimately God has created a unique journey for you, and it is only by listening to his voice that you will discover the indescribable joy that comes to us when we finally discover our mission in life.

This joy I have experienced. It is not just an idea. There are two very concrete examples of it in my life. The first is with my work as an author and a speaker. There are many things I could be doing, but I know this is the thing that God wants me to be doing—that he created me for. How do I know? It's hard to describe. When you find your thing, you just know. There is a joy and a timelessness that you experience. You love doing it, even though it isn't always fun; you lose track of time when you are hard at work; and you have a deep peace within you, which comes from the sense that this is the thing for you to dedicate your life to. I want you to discover and experience that.

The other area of my life where I experience this joy is in my marriage. I have lived away from Australia for almost twenty years now. But every time I fly into Sydney, and see the Harbour Bridge and the Opera House, I still get the same feeling. It is the feeling of arriving home. I travel a lot for work, and there is something wonderful about coming home. When I met Meggie I had that feeling. When I married her I had that feeling, the feeling that I was finally home. Whatever vocation God calls you to, I want you to experience that same feeling of arriving home after a long journey.

I can't tell you what your mission in life is, but I can tell you two things that will flawlessly help you to discover it.

1) While you may not know the specifics of your mission, you do know your mission in a broad sense, because it is the same for us all. Your mission is to make the love of God known to the world. In your own place and time, in your own ways, you are here to bring the love of God to every person who crosses your path.

2) Do the next right thing. The surest way to discover your mission is to do what you know to be the right thing, right now. If you do the next right thing often enough for long enough, you will live your way into the incredible life that God has designed just for you.

JOURNAL QUESTION

1. WHAT ARE YOU AFRAID OF?

2. ONE DAY, WHEN YOU ARE DYING, WHAT DO YOU WANT TO SEE W LOOK BACK ON YOUR LIFE?

3. HOW AVAILABLE ARE YOU TO GOD?

WATCH VIDEO

11.5 DECISION point

3 MIN

> **Tip**
>
> Ask them if they are open to whatever mission God has for them.

EXERCISE: Know It. Think About It. Live It.

TIP

Ask someone to read aloud the Bible passage highlighted in the section **KNOW IT. THINK ABOUT IT. LIVE IT.** Ask another student to read the text from the workbook. [WB276]

Discuss the story of the Good Samaritan. Explore ways the candidates can be like the Good Samaritan in their everyday lives.

5 MIN

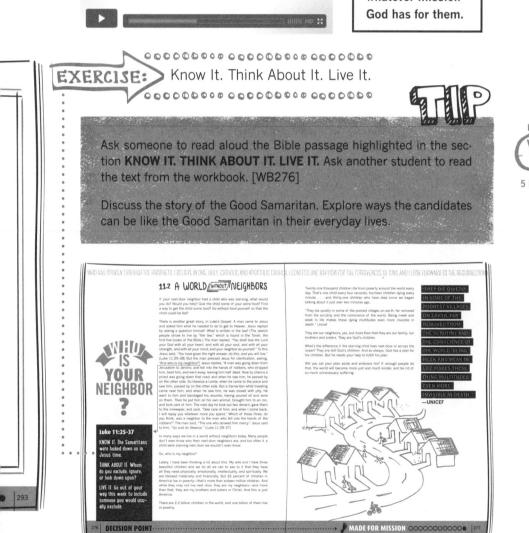

11.2 A WORLD WITHOUT NEIGHBORS

If your next-door neighbor had a child who was starving, what would you do? Would you help? Give the child some of your extra food? Find a way to get the child some food? Go without food yourself so that the child could be fed?

There is another great story, in Luke's Gospel. A man came to Jesus and asked him what he needed to do to get to Heaven. Jesus replied by asking a question himself: What is written in the law? (The Jewish people strove to live by "the law," which is found in the Torah, the first five books of the Bible.) The man replied, "You shall love the Lord your God with all your heart, and with all your soul, and with all your strength, and with all your mind; and your neighbor as yourself." To this Jesus said, "You have given the right answer; do this, and you will live." (Luke 11:25–28) But the man pressed Jesus for clarification, asking, "And who is my neighbor?" Jesus replied, "A man was going down from Jerusalem to Jericho, and fell into the hands of robbers, who stripped him, beat him, and went away, leaving him half dead. Now by chance a priest was going down that road; and when he saw him, he passed by on the other side. So likewise a Levite, when he came to the place and saw him, passed by on the other side. But a Samaritan while traveling came near him; and when he saw him, he was moved with pity. He went to him and bandaged his wounds, having poured oil and wine on them. Then he put him on his own animal, brought him to an inn, and took care of him. The next day he took out two denarii, gave them to the innkeeper, and said, 'Take care of him; and when I come back, I will repay you whatever more you spend.' Which of these three, do you think, was a neighbor to the man who fell into the hands of the robbers?" The man said, "The one who showed him mercy." Jesus said to him, "Go and do likewise." (Luke 11:29–37)

In many ways we live in a world without neighbors today. Many people don't even know who their next-door neighbors are, and too often if a child were starving next door we wouldn't even know.

So, who is my neighbor?

Lately, I have been thinking a lot about this. My wife and I have three beautiful children and we do all we can to see to it that they have all they need physically, emotionally, intellectually, and spiritually. We are blessed materially and financially. But 22 percent of children in America live in poverty—that's more than sixteen million children. And while they may not live next door, they are my neighbors—and more than that, they are my brothers and sisters in Christ. And this is just America.

There are 2.2 billion children in the world, and one billion of them live in poverty.

Twenty-one thousand children die from poverty around the world every day. That's one child every four seconds, fourteen children dying every minute . . . and thirty-one children who have died since we began talking about it just over two minutes ago.

"They die quietly in some of the poorest villages on earth, far removed from the scrutiny and the conscience of the world. Being meek and weak in life makes these dying multitudes even more invisible in death." Unicef

They are our neighbors, yes, but more than that they are our family, our brothers and sisters. They are God's children.

What's the difference if the starving child lives next door or across the ocean? They are still God's children. And as always, God has a plan for his children. But he needs your help to fulfill his plan.

Will you set your plan aside and embrace his? If enough people do that, the world will become more just and much kinder, and be rid of so much unnecessary suffering.

> "THEY DIE QUIETLY IN SOME OF THE POOREST VILLAGES ON EARTH, FAR REMOVED FROM THE SCRUTINY AND THE CONSCIENCE OF THE WORLD. BEING MEEK AND WEAK IN LIFE MAKES THESE DYING MULTITUDES EVEN MORE INVISIBLE IN DEATH."
> —UNICEF

WHO IS YOUR NEIGHBOR?

Luke 11:25-37

KNOW IT: The Samaritans were looked down on in Jesus time.

THINK ABOUT IT: Whom do you exclude, ignore, or look down upon?

LIVE IT: Go out of your way this week to include someone you would usually exclude.

293

STEP 4 JOURNAL

8 MIN

INSTRUCTIONS: It's time to journal. This time is sacred; remind them of that. Invite your class to open up to page 293 and take a few minutes in silence to journal their answers to those questions.

TIP

If we are not accustomed to this type of reflection, the journaling process can be difficult, even painful. But the rewards for doing this kind of work cannot be overstated. They reach into every aspect of our lives, by making us more aware of who we are and what we are here for.

STEP 5 ANNOUNCEMENTS

3 MIN

Tip

Thank them for coming. Never stop thanking them for coming.

Tell them you enjoyed your time with them. Talk about something during the class that made you think or laugh.

Remind them you are praying for them.

Encourage them to watch the short films again during the week online or on the app.

TIP

Before you read the Psalm today, encourage the class to sit still and quiet for a couple of minutes and just listen to whatever God is saying to them.

Close with a spontaneous prayer asking God to bless these young people and help them discover the mission he has designed just for them.

5 MIN

PSALM 141

I call upon thee, O Lord; make haste to me!
Give ear to my voice, when I call to thee!

² Let my prayer be counted as incense before thee,
and the lifting up of my hands as an evening sacrifice!

³ Set a guard over my mouth, O Lord,
keep watch over the door of my lips!

⁴ Incline not my heart to any evil,
to busy myself with wicked deeds
in company with men who work iniquity;
and let me not eat of their dainties!

⁵ Let a good man strike or rebuke me in kindness,
but let the oil of the wicked never anoint my head;
for my prayer is continually against their wicked deeds.

⁶ When they are given over to those who shall condemn them,
then they shall learn that the word of the Lord is true.

⁷ As a rock which one cleaves and shatters on the land,
so shall their bones be strewn at the mouth of Sheol.

⁸ But my eyes are toward thee, O Lord God;
in thee I seek refuge; leave me not defenseless!

⁹ Keep me from the trap which they have laid for me,
and from the snares of evildoers!

¹⁰ Let the wicked together fall
into their own nets, while I escape.

284 **DECISION POINT** .... ▶ **MADE FOR MISSION** ○○○○

HOLINESS
is possible

We thank you for this day and for all your blessings. Help us to remain always grateful for all you do for us and in us. Watch over in a special way today anyone who is hungry, lonely, depressed, addicted, unemployed, or just in need of the human touch, and inspire us to realize that we are your partners in the work you wish to do in the world. Help us to remain ever mindful of the great love you have for each and every one of us, and give us the courage to respond with the bold enthusiasm of a little child. We ask all this in Jesus' name. Amen.

Matthew Kelly

QUICK SESSION OVERVIEW

STEP 1	**WELCOME**
STEP 2	**OPENING PRAYER**
STEP 3	**ENGAGE – WATCH & DISCUSS**
STEP 4	**JOURNAL**
STEP 5	**ANNOUNCEMENTS**
STEP 6	**CLOSING PRAYER**

SESSION TWELVE: HOLINESS IS POSSIBLE

Objectives:

- To help candidates recognize that there is a connection between happiness and holiness.

- To demonstrate that holiness is possible.

- To teach candidates how to say yes to God and that their yes can make a huge difference.

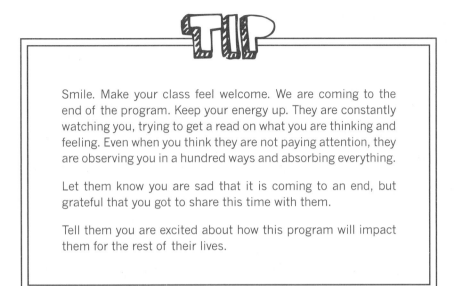

Smile. Make your class feel welcome. We are coming to the end of the program. Keep your energy up. They are constantly watching you, trying to get a read on what you are thinking and feeling. Even when you think they are not paying attention, they are observing you in a hundred ways and absorbing everything.

Let them know you are sad that it is coming to an end, but grateful that you got to share this time with them.

Tell them you are excited about how this program will impact them for the rest of their lives.

LEADER GUIDE KEY

TIME-ICON: This icon serves as a guide to help you plan approximately how long each activity will take.

[WB5] This code serves as a reference to point you to the page in the Workbook where you can find the related activity/content.

Example: **[WB5]** *points you to page 5 in the Workbook*

The flag icon is the halfway mark and suggests a good breaking point if your program runs twenty-four classes (or approximately 60 minutes) instead of twelve 120 minute classes.

STEP 2 OPENING PRAYER

· · · · · · · · · · · · · · · · · ·

Tip

Take a moment to get them quiet.

Now, speak to the candidates about why quiet time is important in our lives. Encourage them to continue the habit of taking a few quiet minutes in prayer each day for the rest of their lives. Remind them that there are going to be tough times in their lives, there are going to be times when they are confused, and at those times in particular you would encourage them to turn to God in prayer and ask him to guide them.

Begin with the Sign of the Cross, invite them to close their eyes, and read the opening prayer slowly and deliberately. Then give them thirty seconds in silence to reflect on the prayer and what God is saying to them through it.

3 MIN

We thank you for this day and for all your blessings. Help us to remain always grateful for all you do for us and in us. Watch over in a special way today anyone who is hungry, lonely, depressed, addicted, unemployed, or just in need of the human touch, and inspire us to realize that we are your partners in the work you wish to do in the world. Help us to remain ever mindful of the great love you have for each and every one of us, and give us the courage to respond with the bold enthusiasm of a little child. We ask all this in Jesus' name. Amen.

Matthew Kelly

SESSION 12 INTRODUCTION

WATCH VIDEO

4 MIN

TIP:

Whatever it is we feel called to accomplish in this life requires perseverance. Tell them they are about to hear one of the greatest stories of perseverance. Tell them about a time when you were tempted to quit, but you felt God encouraging you to persevere. Explain why you are glad you did.

DISCUSSION QUESTION

4 MIN

1) What is the one idea in this short film that you found most helpful?

SESSION 12.1 THE HOLY MOMENT

WATCH VIDEO

7 MIN

DISCUSSION QUESTIONS [WB301]

10 MIN

Tip The biggest Christian lie in history is not one that others tell about us. It is a lie we tell ourselves: Holiness is not possible. This lie neutralizes our Christianity. It is diabolical. Holiness *is* possible.

1) Who is the holiest person you know? What makes that person holy?

2) Who is your favorite saint? Why?

3) What's one thing you have learned throughout the DECISION POINT experience that surprised you?

Invite a student to read aloud **"Who Was David?"** Discuss how David's heart was like the heart of God. Explore how our hearts are capable of expressing themselves like God does, with love, mercy, compassion, generosity, and forgiveness.   [WB310]

TIP!

Do you know everyone's name in the class? Use their names. Let them know that you know who they are and that you are glad you were able to share this journey with them.

HE WILL COME AGAIN IN GLORY TO JUDGE THE LIVING AND THE DEAD AND HIS KINGDOM WILL HAVE NO END.

WHO WAS DAVID?

David was an ancestor of Jesus (c. 1040 BC–970 BC) and perhaps the most brilliant leader of ancient Israel. He had the mind and charisma to inspire a great nation. In other ways he was a very ordinary man who struggled with destructive passion and was motivated at times by political gain. Yet through it all he had a deep love of God. The Bible describes David as a man after God's own heart (Acts 13:22).

When David was just a boy he was summoned to play music for King Saul in order to cure his melancholy. David also gained fame in his youth when he killed the Philistine Goliath with his slingshot. After Saul died, David rose to power and became King of Israel, uniting the twelve tribes.

the pledge. Read it slowly, pray about it, and sign it. Say yes to God and his Church, and say yes enthusiastically. Not just a whimpering, passive yes, but a wholehearted and enthusiastic YES.

Your Catholic faith will always be a part of you. You get to decide if it is going to be something powerful and positive, or something negative and misunderstood.

God has a plan. When we don't play our part, the whole thing falls apart. It's all connected. Imagine if Mary had said no. Her yes has touched every person who has lived for two thousand years. You see, every decision made by every person echoes down through history.

Sometimes I wonder if the reason we don't have a cure for cancer, AIDS, and Alzheimer's is because the people who were going to find those cures were among the fifty-five million children who have been aborted in the United States since *Roe v. Wade*. God had a plan for every one of those children, just as he has a plan for you. You have a part to play in God's plan for the world.

You might be tempted to think, "Oh, I'm nobody special; God doesn't have any special plans for me." But that would be a mistake. Read Chapter 17 of the first book of Samuel for a great example. David's father sent him to take food to his brothers, who were in the army. When he got there Goliath, the enormous and much feared Philistine, was daring the Israelites to fight him, but they were all too afraid. David said to king Saul, "I'll fight him." Saul told him he could not because David, who was little more than a child, was too young. David and Saul went back and forth and finally the king agreed. The rest is history. David slew Goliath, and in time God made this lowly shepherd boy the king of his people.

David made himself available.

God uses the most unlikely people to do his greatest work. As you read the Bible, you'll discover that he almost never uses those in positions of power and authority; he doesn't necessarily use the most educated, or the best looking, or even the most qualified. Whom does God use to do his most powerful work here on earth? He uses the people who make themselves available to him. How available are you to God? Ten percent, 50 percent, 95 percent? Or are you 100 percent available for whatever God calls you to today?

Want to see something truly incredible? Make yourself available to God.

DISCUSSION QUESTIONS

1. ARE YOU READY TO LET GOD COME AND FILL YOU UP IN ALL THE WAYS YOU NEED AND WANT TO BE FILLED?

2. WHAT HAVE YOU SAID YES TO IN THE PAST THAT YOU KNEW WAS NOT FOR YOU?

3. HOW AVAILABLE ARE YOU TO GOD TODAY?

310 | DECISION POINT ....▶ HOLINESS IS POSSIBLE ○○○○○○○○○○○○ | 311

6 MIN

SESSION 12.2 EVERYTHING IS AN OPPORTUNITY

WATCH VIDEO

12.2 Everything IS AN Opportunity

> **T I P**
>
> The closer you get to the end, the more restless some of your students will become. Be prepared for that; have techniques at the ready. Take a break and play a song or a game. Think of ways to actively keep them engaged until the end.

10 MIN

DISCUSSION QUESTIONS [WB306]

1) Who do you know who does little things with great love?

2) What little things can you do with great love today?

3) What does today's culture think about doing little things with great love?

SESSION 12.3 YOUR YES CAN CHANGE THE WORLD

WATCH VIDEO

12.3 your YES can change the WORLD

🕐
10 MIN

TIP

Everything is an opportunity. Very often the biggest opportunities in life are draped in the very ordinary things of life. It is only in looking back that we realize God was using the most basic circumstances to bring about his beautiful plan for our lives.

Your candidates have a very compressed understanding of time. Expand their vision by talking about different stages of your life, and how quickly time passes.

DISCUSSION QUESTIONS [WB311]

10 MIN

1) Are you ready to let God come and fill you up in all the ways you need and want to be filled?

2) What have you said yes to in the past that you knew was not for you?

3) How available are you to God today?

EXERCISE:

5 MIN

Tip

Ask them to write a letter to themselves about the experience on the My Thoughts page of their workbook.

discussion questions

OU KNOW WHO DOES LITTLE THINGS WITH GREAT LOVE?

'LE THINGS CAN YOU DO WITH GREAT LOVE TODAY?

'S TODAY'S CULTURE THINK ABOUT DOING LITTLE THINGS WITH GREAT LOVE?

MY THOUGHTS

ON POINT

▶ ⏳ HOLINESS IS POSSIBLE ○○○○○○○○○○○○ | 307

SESSION 12.4 **REVIEW**

WATCH VIDEO

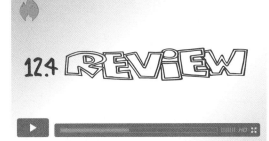

7 MIN

TIP · · · · · · · · ·

Pay attention, candidates. You are about to review the whole program in seven minutes.

DISCUSSION QUESTIONS [WB318]

10 MIN

1) What new habit have you developed since you started this program?

2) What is the best idea you heard during the entire experience?

3) What is one thing you can do this week to better prepare yourself for Confirmation?

EXERCISE VIRTUE IN FOCUS

4 MIN

TIP

This session highlights the virtue of chastity. Invite someone to read aloud the **Virtue in Focus** section. Choose one of the questions from the section and encourage the candidates to share their answers. [WB320]

WHO WITH THE FATHER AND THE SON IS ADORED AND GLORIFIED, WHO HAS SPOKEN THROUGH THE PROPHETS. I BELIEVE IN ONE, HOLY, CATHOLIC AND APOSTOLIC CHURCH. I CON

12.5 DREAM!

As human beings we have many fabulous abilities, but God has bestowed on us two truly incredible gifts. The first is free will. We each have the ability to choose. The second is the ability to dream. Unlike any of the other creatures that God created, we can look into the future, imagine something better in the future, and then come back to the present and work in the present to bring about the future we have envisioned. Our ability to dream is an astounding gift.

So, what are your dreams? What dreams has God placed in your heart? You see, your dreams are your dreams for a reason. God has given us the ability to dream and placed certain dreams for good things in each of our hearts. What are your dreams? And what are you doing about them?

When I was a teenager I had a great soccer coach, but he was really tough on us. One day I got up in his face and screamed at him, "What do you want from me?" He looked at me calmly and said, "What do you want for yourself?"

Throughout your life there will be many people who want something from you. There will be relatively few who want absolutely nothing from you.

I don't want anything from you, but there are some things I want *for* you. I want you to experience the love of God in ways so powerful that you cannot resist embracing him with your whole heart, mind, and soul. I want you to become all he created you to be—the-very-best-version-of-yourself. I want you to experience the incredible joy that comes from saying yes to God and placing Jesus at the center of your life. I want you to be astounded by the genius of Catholicism. And after a long, full, and happy life filled with love, laughter, and dreams come true, I want you to die well and spend all of eternity with God in Heaven.

For four years I have been praying for you every day. And I am going to keep praying for you each day for the rest of my life. I pray that you have the courage and the wisdom to make these things we have discussed part of your life, and I pray that in your own way you will bring the love of God to others as they cross your path.

This time with you has been an honor. Thank you for allowing me to make this journey with you. I hope our paths cross again soon.

WHAT DREAMS HAS GOD PLACED IN YOUR HEART?

VIRTUE IN FOCUS

Chas·ti·ty
[chas-i-tee]

sexual purity and self-control in thought, intention, and conduct

Why is chastity important?

What does the culture try to tell you about chastity?

What can you do to rebel against what the culture says about chastity?

When I got married I was thirty-five years old, and for fifteen years I had been on the road, traveling from one city to the next. One of the things that I love about being married is that I have someone to pray with. There is something wonderful and powerful about praying with other people. Jesus said, "Wherever two or more are gathered in my name, I am there among them."(Matthew 18:20) Here we are, gathered in Jesus' name. If it weren't for him, we wouldn't be here right now. So let us close our eyes, and end our time together with prayer:

Loving Father,

We thank you for this day and for all your blessings.

Help us to remain always grateful for all you do for us and in us,

watch over in a special way today anyone who is hungry, lonely, depressed, addicted, unemployed, or just in need of the human touch,

and inspire us to realize that we are your partners in the work you wish to do in the world.

Help us to remain ever mindful of the great love you have for each and every one of us, and give us the courage to respond with the bold enthusiasm of a little child.

We ask all this in Jesus' name as we pray as he taught us to.

Our Father . . .

On behalf of everyone at Dynamic Catholic, I want to thank you for participating in this journey toward Confirmation. We hope we can serve you in powerful ways throughout your life. Don't let this be the end. Make a commitment to do something every day for the rest of your life that will help you grow spiritually. And I look forward to meeting you somewhere along the way as our pilgrimage continues...

320 | **DECISION POINT** ⋯⋯⋯⋯⋯⋯⋯⋯⋯⋯⋯⋯⋯⋯⋯⋯⋯⋯⋯⋯⋯⋯⋯► ⧖ **HOLINESS IS POSSIBLE** ○○○○

SESSION 12.5 DREAM!

WATCH VIDEO

Tip

This is video number seventy-two, the last one. Are you ready?

5 MIN

EXERCISE: Know It. Think About It. Live It.

TIP

Ask someone to read aloud the Bible passage highlighted in the section **KNOW IT. THINK ABOUT IT. LIVE IT.** Ask another student to read the text from the workbook. [WB308]

Discuss what their concept of holiness is and how that is different from what has been presented throughout this program.

5 MIN

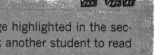

HE WILL COME AGAIN IN GLORY TO JUDGE THE LIVING AND THE DEAD AND HIS KINGDOM WILL HAVE NO END. I BELIEVE IN THE HOLY SPIRIT, THE LORD, THE GIVER OF LIFE, WHO PROCEEDS FROM THE FATHER AND

12.3 your YES can change the WORLD

WHAT ARE YOU *trying to* **FILL YOUR EMPTINESS** —*with?*—

1 Thessalonians 5:17 "pray constantly"

KNOW IT: We are called to transform every moment into a prayer.

THINK ABOUT IT: How can you transform your daily activity into prayer? For whom can you offer these prayers to God?

LIVE IT: Offer each hour of work of study to God as a prayer for a specific intention.

Throughout your life there are going to be times when you feel like there must be more to life or that something is missing. We all have the same kind of empty feeling from time to time. You see, we all have a hole in us that needs to be filled.

We try to fill that hole in lots of different ways. When I was a child I thought the hole would be filled if Santa brought me just what I wanted or if I won enough soccer games and golf matches. As I grew older I tried to fill that hole with other things.

We try to fill the hole with pleasure, but that doesn't work. We tell ourselves, "Maybe I can fill it with stuff!" So we get a car, a house, clothes, a watch, handbags, jewelry, shoes—everything the material world has to offer. But that doesn't fill the hole either, and the empty feeling remains. So we go off to see the world and find ourselves, but that doesn't fill the hole. Next we chase accomplishment. "If I can just achieve enough, perhaps that will fill the hole." We achieve great things, but the emptiness continues to reign. The hole is still there.

We are slow learners, so we usually cycle through several rounds of each of these attempts at filling the hole. More pleasure, more travel, more stuff, more accomplishments, the right friends, sex, drugs, fame, status . . . but time and time again the emptiness continues. In fact, the more you try to fill the hole with these things, the bigger the hole seems to be.

We all experience the same kind of emptiness. Why? The reason is profoundly simple. We each have a God-sized hole in us. Only God can fill the hole. Try anything else you want, but it won't work. It never has and it never will.

My favorite line in the Catechism is the opening line in Chapter One, which reads: "The desire for God is written in the human heart, because man is created by God and for God, and God never ceases to draw man to himself. Only in God will he find the truth and the happiness he never stops searching for."

You have a God-sized hole in you. What are you trying to fill it with? Are you ready to let God take away that emptiness once and for all? Life is choices. You get to decide.

It's amazing how a simple yes or no can change your life.

One of the most practical things about growing spiritually is that we get really good at saying no. Most people are bad at saying no. Every day we find ourselves saying yes to things that we know we should be

saying no to. We do this because of peer pressure, fear of missing out on something, a false feeling of obligation, or just to stay busy so we can distract ourselves from really thinking about life and what God is calling us to. But here's the thing: When we say yes to stuff we know is not for us, we miss out on the stuff that is uniquely ours.

Let me give you an example. I was talking to a friend of mine the other day and I asked him how his girlfriend, Julie, was. He said she was great, so I asked him if he thought she was the one for him. He said no. So I asked him when they were going to break up. He said they weren't going to break up. I asked why and he said that he really liked her and they had fun together.

"What are you doing Friday night?" I asked.

"Taking Julie to that new movie."

On Friday night, when he was out at the movies with Julie, that might have been the night when he was going to meet the woman that God had created just for him. When we say yes to stuff that is not for us, we miss out on the stuff that God created just for us.

Get really good at saying no to anything that you know is not for you. And the only way to say no to anything, is to have a deeper yes. As we grow spiritually – through prayer, the Scriptures, and the Sacraments – we get really clear about: who we are, what we are here for, what matters most, and what matters least. This personal clarity allows us to be really good at say yes to the right things and no to the stuff that just isn't part of God's plan for us.

If you have been practicing The Prayer Process each day I'm sure you are already getting a clearer sense of who you are, what you're here for, what matters most, and what matters least. And that personal clarity is a beautiful thing.

From the beginning it has been my hope that this program will help you become a great decision maker, because decision making is so central to our experience of life. Learning to say yes to the right things and no to the wrong things is essential.

Now it's time to face the decision at hand. At baptism your parents and godparents made a choice for you. Now you have to decide for yourself—and make no mistake, it is one of the biggest decisions of your life. God has chosen you. The question is: How will you respond?

We have been making this journey toward Confirmation, and now we are almost there. It's time to commit. Say yes to Confirmation, but much more than that, decide today to say yes to Jesus and his Church. Choose them, for they have chosen you. Open your workbooks and sign

"WHAT YOU ARE IS GOD'S GIFT TO YOU. WHAT YOU BECOME IS YOUR GIFT TO GOD."

HANS URS VON BALTHASAR

100% AVAILABLE

STEP 4 JOURNAL

8 MIN

INSTRUCTIONS: It's time to journal. This time is sacred; remind them of that. Invite your class to open up to page 322 and take a few minutes in silence to journal their answers to those questions.

TIP

Take a moment to mention how the journaling process has helped you grow. Encourage them to continue to journal once a week for the rest of their lives. Tell them how fascinating it is to look back and read what you wrote a year ago or ten years ago.

STEP 5 ANNOUNCEMENTS

3 MIN

Tip

Thank them for coming.

Tell them you have enjoyed your time with them.

Talk about the highlights of the program: Funny moments. Serious moments. Life-changing moments.

Remind them you will be praying for them for the rest of their lives.

Encourage them to continue to explore their faith. Promise them that the day will come when they will be glad they took this stuff seriously.

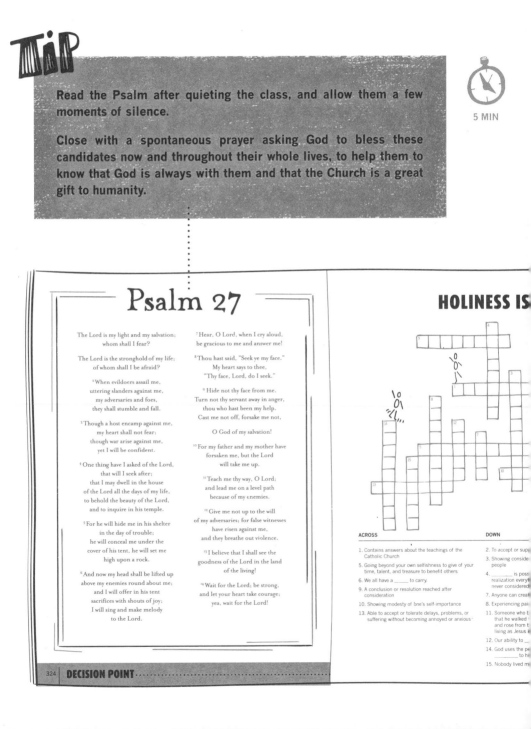

TIP

Read the Psalm after quieting the class, and allow them a few moments of silence.

Close with a spontaneous prayer asking God to bless these candidates now and throughout their whole lives, to help them to know that God is always with them and that the Church is a great gift to humanity.

5 MIN

Psalm 27

The Lord is my light and my salvation;
whom shall I fear?

The Lord is the stronghold of my life;
of whom shall I be afraid?

²When evildoers assail me,
uttering slanders against me,
my adversaries and foes,
they shall stumble and fall.

³Though a host encamp against me,
my heart shall not fear;
though war arise against me,
yet I will be confident.

⁴One thing have I asked of the Lord,
that will I seek after;
that I may dwell in the house
of the Lord all the days of my life,
to behold the beauty of the Lord,
and to inquire in his temple.

⁵For he will hide me in his shelter
in the day of trouble;
he will conceal me under the
cover of his tent, he will set me
high upon a rock.

⁶And now my head shall be lifted up
above my enemies round about me;
and I will offer in his tent
sacrifices with shouts of joy;
I will sing and make melody
to the Lord.

⁷Hear, O Lord, when I cry aloud,
be gracious to me and answer me!

⁸Thou hast said, "Seek ye my face."
My heart says to thee,
"Thy face, Lord, do I seek."

⁹Hide not thy face from me.
Turn not thy servant away in anger,
thou who hast been my help.
Cast me not off, forsake me not,

O God of my salvation!

¹⁰For my father and my mother have
forsaken me, but the Lord
will take me up.

¹¹Teach me thy way, O Lord;
and lead me on a level path
because of my enemies.

¹²Give me not up to the will
of my adversaries; for false witnesses
have risen against me,
and they breathe out violence.

¹³I believe that I shall see the
goodness of the Lord in the land
of the living!

¹⁴Wait for the Lord; be strong,
and let your heart take courage;
yea, wait for the Lord!

HOLINESS IS

ACROSS

1. Contains answers about the teachings of the Catholic Church
5. Going beyond your own selfishness to give of your time, talent, and treasure to benefit others
6. We all have a _____ to carry.
9. A conclusion or resolution reached after consideration
10. Showing modesty of one's self-importance
13. Able to accept or tolerate delays, problems, or suffering without becoming annoyed or anxious

DOWN

2. To accept or supp
3. Showing conside people
4. _____ is poss realization every never considered
7. Anyone can crea
8. Experiencing pai
11. Someone who b that he walked and rose from t living as Jesus
12. Our ability to _
14. God uses the pe _____ to hi
15. Nobody lived m

MY THOUGHTS

MY THOUGHTS

MY THOUGHTS

My Thoughts

MY
THOUGHTS

MY THOUGHTS

My Thoughts